Picturing
the Project Approach

Creative Explorations in Early Learning

Sylvia Chard, Yvonne Kogan, Carmen Castillo

Gryphon House

www.gryphonhouse.com

Published by Gryphon House, Inc.

P. O. Box 10, Lewisville, NC 27023

800.638.0928; fax 877.638.7576

www.gryphonhouse.com

Photographs courtesy of the authors and their educator colleagues and friends in various countries.

Bulk Purchase

Gryphon House books are available for special premiums and sales promotions as well as for fund-raising use. Special editions or book excerpts also can be created to specifications. For details, call 800.638.0928.

Disclaimer

Gryphon House, Inc., cannot be held responsible for damage, mishap, or injury incurred during the use of or because of activities in this book. Appropriate and reasonable caution and adult supervision of children involved in activities and corresponding to the age and capability of each child involved are recommended at all times. Do not leave children unattended at any time. Observe safety and caution at all times.

Reprinted March 2020

Library of Congress Cataloging-in-Publication Data

Names: Kogan, Yvonne, author.
Title: Picturing the project approach : creative explorations in early
   learning / by Yvonne Kogan, Sylvia Chard, Carmen A. Castillo.
Description: Lewisville, NC : Gryphon House Inc., [2017]
Identifiers: LCCN 2017013513 (print) | LCCN 2017036664 (ebook) | ISBN
   9780876595732 () | ISBN 9780876595725 (paperback)
Subjects: LCSH: Project method in teaching. | BISAC: EDUCATION / Preschool &
   Kindergarten.
Classification: LCC LB1139.35.P8 (ebook) | LCC LB1139.35.P8 K64 2017 (print)
   | DDC 371.3/6--dc23
LC record available at https://lccn.loc.gov/2017013513

Dedications

To my husband, David Miall, and all my wonderful family.

—Sylvia C. Chard

To Sammy, who continues to fill my days with love; to my children, the driving force in my life; and to my grandchildren, who are certainly "the cherry on the cake."

—Yvonne Kogan

A mis adorados Juanitos, pues ellos tres siempre serán la fuente de mi inspiración.

—Carmen A. Castillo

Contents

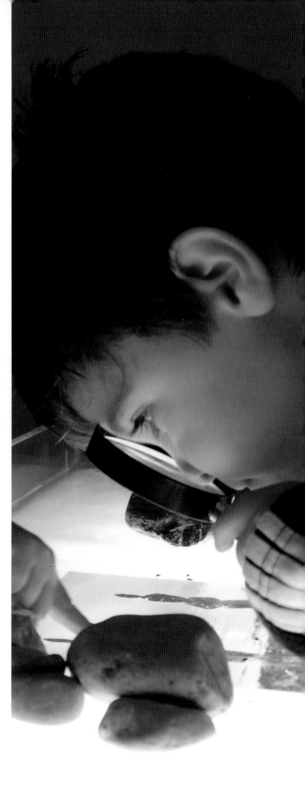

Foreword

Involving young children in investigations that we refer to as "projects" first emerged in the United States almost a century ago. The educational philosophers and scholars John Dewey and William Kilpatrick were among several who alerted educators to the importance of engaging children's minds more fully than did formal traditional teaching methods.

This book provides rich descriptions and illustrations of projects undertaken by young children in many parts of the world. As young children engage in the wide variety of project activities documented here, teachers, parents and family members, and the larger community being served can appreciate three of the main premises underlying these educational practices, outlined briefly below.

My extensive experience in teaching young children suggests that it is useful to keep in mind the following assumptions based on research about children's development and learning. Furthermore, I encourage you to share these assumptions with their families.

First, one way of looking at the risks of excessive formal instruction is to keep in mind the distinctions between academic and intellectual goals and activities, especially during the early years. Academic goals are those concerned with acquiring small, discrete bits of information, usually related to preliteracy skills. Academic activities tend to involve drills, worksheets, and other kinds of exercises designed to prepare the children for later literacy and numeracy learning and uses. The items learned and practiced require correct answers and rely heavily on memorization versus understanding. Academic exercises consist largely of giving the teacher the correct answers that the children know she is waiting for them to provide. For young children, such academic activities include learning the days of the week. Although one of the traditional meanings of the term *academic* is "of little practical value or relevance," these bits of information are essential components of reading and other academic competencies that ultimately become important. I suggest that the issue here is not whether academic skills matter. Rather, the questions are: When do they matter? And how much do they matter at what ages?

Intellectual goals and their related activities, on the other hand, address the life of the mind in its fullest sense, including a range of aesthetic sensitivities. The concept of *intellectual* emphasizes reasoning, hypothesizing, predicting, analyzing, imagining, developing ideas, and engaging in a quest for understanding. An appropriate curriculum for young children focuses on supporting their inborn intellectual dispositions. For example, children are naturally disposed to make the best sense they can of their own experience and environment. An appropriate curriculum in the early years is one that encourages and motivates children to seek mastery of basic academic skills, such as beginning writing skills, in the service of their intellectual pursuits. The children become more able to sense the purposefulness of their academic activities and efforts as they pursue their interests and observations. Thus, even young children engaged in various aspects of a project investigation and documentation learn a great deal, as teachers facilitate their efforts to measure relevant phenomena and to write down a variety of words and numbers. In this way, they deepen their awareness of the uses of academic skills.

Another important aspect of development and learning that applies to project work is that it addresses the distinctions between excitement and interest. There are many occasions in the lives of young children when excitement occurs and is welcomed, such as birthday parties, holiday celebrations, and various kinds of play and games. In contrast, interest is a kind of slowing down of physical reactions and a strengthening of mental processing of ideas and events. Interest, which may appear as deep absorption, curiosity, and even fascination, is essential to aspects of extended project work throughout the early years.

A third distinction of project work is that its value is based on the experiences the children have as they undertake the varied activities and work involved. Among the values embedded in good project work are intellectual and social experiences. Project work is not designed around anticipated questions that are intended to address academic outcomes assessed in formal tests and examinations.

As can be seen in the reports and pictures of project work in this book, the children and their teachers are deeply engaged in their investigations and in providing documentation of what they are accomplishing. This book provides ample evidence of the many benefits project work offers our young children throughout their development.

—Lilian G. Katz, PhD, professor emerita, elementary and early childhood education, University of Illinois

Preface

During many years of working with teachers of young children, we have found that a large number of them want to change their teaching practices so that they are more aligned with the demands of our times. Furthermore, teachers are often looking toward the future and are seriously reconsidering issues concerning what and how children should be learning at school. In these processes of individual and collaborative reflection, educators have frequently expressed interest in learning how to guide young children in developing skills and dispositions that will be universally valuable across places and times. This book provides you with step-by-step guidelines in using the project approach as a framework to enrich your practice, by planning educational experiences that nurture the lively minds of children. It illustrates how social-emotional development; academic benchmarks; and science, technology, engineering, and math (STEM) knowledge and skills are promoted in the context of a project. Additionally, this book offers a section about tools that includes templates and sample letters that you may consult and use throughout the course of project work. Its text and powerful, captivating images complement each other to facilitate understanding as you implement the project approach in your classroom.

Acknowledgments

We first and foremost want to thank Dr. Lilian Katz, who, along with Dr. Sylvia Chard, has developed the project approach and has written extensively about it in books, articles, and papers, has lectured all around the world, and has mentored teachers and institutions in implementing practices that make learning meaningful.

We also want to acknowledge the work of Carlos Ramírez and of the many teachers who have contributed to this book with their experiences, their stories, and their amazing photographs, all of which bring the project approach to life.

1 Understanding the Project Approach

A project is an extended and in-depth investigation of a real-world topic. Children gain deep understanding and knowledge by seeking answers to their questions through rich sensory, firsthand investigations. Projects are usually undertaken by a whole class, divided into small groups. These groups become experts in different aspects of the topic of study.

The project approach is not the whole curriculum and is compatible with and complementary to other experiences and instructional methods. Teachers of young children often wonder about the distinction between a thematic unit and a project. Table 1.1 highlights several differences. Note that with thematic units, teachers preplan from beginning to end. With a project, teachers respond to the children's ideas, and the unit's progression follows children's interests to achieve goals that the class members have set together.

The project approach provides a well-structured, user-friendly framework involving three phases. Like a good story, the project can be described as having a beginning, a middle, and an end, each memorable in its own way. The organization of projects into three sequential phases helps teachers and children identify the purposefulness of the work as it unfolds.

Table 1.1: Distinctions between Thematic Units and Projects

Element	Thematic Units	Projects
Topic	This usually refers to a set of activities around a broad topic or large concept, such as the solar system.	This involves a piece of in-depth research about a real-world topic that is close to the children's lives, such as shoes.
Duration	The duration of thematic units is usually preset and not very long, as this kind of work tends to be superficial.	Projects are longer and may vary considerably in time, depending on the children's continued interest in the topic and on whether they have answered their questions and represented their newly gained understanding.
Role of the Teacher	The teacher acts as a director.	The teacher gives guidance, and children decide how to advance in their own work.
Learning Experiences	The teacher plans activities from beginning to end based on curriculum goals, regardless of the children's interests or questions.	Teachers assess students' prior knowledge, which helps identify questions for research. The learning experiences are designed to allow children to investigate their questions and meet learning and curricular objectives and standards as the project proceeds.
Skills	The teacher finds ways to connect the thematic unit with the curriculum goals. Counting, measuring, reading, spelling, and so forth are used in such a way that the theme serves as a pretext for applying basic skills.	Students meet curriculum objectives as the project progresses. Children apply skills to find answers to their questions and to represent their knowledge and understanding.
Gaining New Knowledge	Information is provided by the teacher mostly from books, manuals, or the Internet. Sometimes children go on a field trip as a culminating activity.	Field visits occur early in the project because this is an essential way for children to find answers to their questions. They also gather firsthand information by conducting interviews; seeing people at work; and examining equipment, places, and processes.
Representation	Children usually engage in the same kinds of activities. They might all color the same worksheet, make a puppet, or take part in a play.	The class is usually divided into interest groups. Children may work independently or collaboratively on varied representations of their new knowledge and understanding related to the questions they investigate. They may produce pieces of writing or drawings, participate in dramatic play, or construct models, among other evidence of learning.
Documentation and Display	Pieces of work may be displayed in the classroom. Because children's thematic work products usually look similar, it is difficult for children to identify their own creations. Display of the work is basically used to decorate the classroom walls.	Teachers document the children's learning process through note taking, photographs, recordings, and videos. They use this documentation to plan subsequent learning experiences. The work displayed reflects the story of the project that is taking place in the classroom and serves as a resource for further learning. Children can easily identify their work, talk about what they learned, and describe the challenges they faced during the project. They feel a true sense of ownership for their individual work products.

Phase 1

At the beginning of the project, the teacher's role is to find out about the firsthand experiences and personal stories that form the basis of individual students' current understanding and what they already know about the topic. Students acquire a collective baseline understanding of the topic through hearing their classmates' stories, representing their own experiences, and sharing their work in class.

Throughout this phase, questions of what the children would like to research are developed in group discussion sessions and become the roadmap for the investigation.

Phase 2

The teacher organizes experiences that allow students to get firsthand information to answer their questions. She brings in objects that youngsters can examine, invites experts to share information with the class, and plans for children to conduct fieldwork. The teacher finds opportunities for students to apply literacy and numeracy skills and acts as a facilitator in helping them represent their new knowledge and understanding in diverse ways.

Phase 3

The teacher, on her own or with her students, decides when and how to conclude the project and how to share the experience with others. The teacher reviews and evaluates the work and usually asks the children to help select particular items for a presentation that will communicate the learning over the course of the project.

Many teachers find it helpful to use a project planning and documentation chart to guide them as they follow the structural features found in each phase, as shown in Table 1.2. The five features of project work—discussion, fieldwork, representation, investigation, and display—serve the children's learning in each phase over the life of the project. As the project progresses through the phases and the teacher's concerns change, each feature of the project work takes on new functions and significance. In appendix A, you can see an example of the project planning and documentation chart filled in with specific items related to a project on fruit.

Table 1.2: Project Planning and Documentation Chart

Discussion	Fieldwork	Representation	Investigation	Display
Phase 1—Beginning the Project				
Sharing prior experience and current knowledge of a topic	Having children talk about their prior experience with their parents and caregivers	Using drawing, writing, construction, and dramatic play to share prior experience and knowledge	Raising questions on the basis of current knowledge	Sharing representations
Phase 2—Developing the Project				
• Preparing for fieldwork and interviews • Reviewing fieldwork • Learning from secondary sources	• Going out of the classroom to investigate a field site • Interviewing experts in the field or in the classroom	• Creating brief field sketches and taking notes • Using drawing, painting, writing, math, diagrams, and maps to represent new learning	• Investigating initial questions • Conducting fieldwork and library research • Raising further questions	• Sharing representations of new experience and knowledge • Keeping ongoing records of the project work
Phase 3—Concluding the Project				
• Preparing to share the story of the project • Reviewing and evaluating the project	Evaluating the project through the eyes of an outside group	Considering and summarizing the story of the study to share the project with others	Speculating about new questions	Summarizing the learning throughout the project

Picturing the Project Approach | Creative Explorations in Early Learning

How Long Should Projects Last?

Projects can last from a few days to several weeks. Short-term projects may arise from an unexpected happening or at the beginning or end of the school term. Longer-term projects are usually grounded on well-selected topics that lend themselves to deeper investigation. Phase 2 takes more time than either phase 1 or phase 3. The time spent on each phase of the project varies according to the age of the children. Younger children should spend a higher percentage of time on phases 1 and 3 than older children spend. For children in preschool to second grade, you would spend about 25 percent of the time on phase 1, 50 percent on phase 2, and 25 percent on phase 3. Those percentages assume that you are conducting a whole-class project.

2 Identifying the Project Topic

At the beginning of a project, the teacher identifies the topic and introduces it to children and families:

- The teacher selects the topic of study.

- The teacher makes a topic web and a curriculum web to envision the potential of the topic.

- The teacher helps children represent their previous experiences in different ways.

- The children share their experiences with their classmates through discussion and displays of their work.

- The teacher informs families about the topic of study so that they may contribute their expertise, send in related objects, and share memories that their child has connected to the topic.

- The teacher identifies and helps the children formulate questions that will guide the investigation.

Selecting the Topic

There are so many interesting things that are part of children's immediate experiences that the potential number of matters to learn about and topics to study is endless. Think of what youngsters encounter and have contact with in their lives every day, from an object as common as a shoe to going to a restaurant; projects provide valuable opportunities for children to gain a deeper understanding of how the world works. Not all topics are equally promising in terms of their educational value. Here are some important issues to consider when selecting a topic:

- Is it of value for the children's learning?

- How can the study of this topic build on what children already know?

- How will it help the children to make better sense of the world in which they live?

- Will the children be able to conduct firsthand, direct investigation by visiting field sites and talking to experts?

- Will it enable students to make sense of literacy and numeracy skills in real-life contexts (depending on the age of the children)?

- Will it meet curriculum standards?

- Will it provide opportunities for collaborative work?

- Will children be able to represent their understanding in different ways?

- Will the children be able to take initiative in pursuing the investigation?

- Will it provide opportunities for family members to become involved in the project?

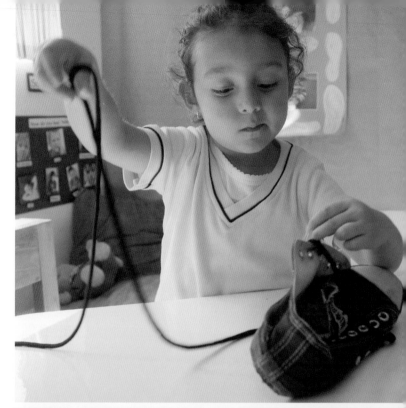

Topics for young children need to be about objects or events that are within their own experience. Among the topics most valuable for toddlers are those that relate to aspects of their daily lives. These may include learning about oneself, water, clothing, pets, or anything that is part of their everyday experience.

Topics for preschool children can relate to familiar places, processes, and objects within their experience. Possibilities include restaurants, airplanes, signs, and the neighborhood around the school.

As children grow through the elementary grades, their interests broaden—as do their experiences with the world—and they become better able to learn about things that are more distant. Good topics for the early elementary grades may include the weather, electricity, or how a newspaper is written, printed, and distributed.

Who Chooses the Topic?

The interests of the children are an important consideration in the selection of the topic. However, asking the children directly what they would like to study may not be the best strategy. Even though appropriate and enriching topics may originate this way, it is the teacher who has the ultimate responsibility of judging whether the topic will be worthy of the children's time and energy.

3

Beginning the Project

Once you have decided on the topic of a project, it is important to make a topic web. In the process of making a topic web or mind map, teachers can gain awareness of their own general knowledge and can envision the potential scope of the topic, the different aspects that may be studied, and the connections to the curriculum.

Making a Topic Web

Focus on including considerable detail in your initial web so that it will be useful for envisioning the class project. A good rule of thumb is for your web to have at least 100 words. The vocabulary should be detailed and suggestive of real-world, everyday language as well as more abstract or conceptual language. (For detailed instructions on how to make a web, see appendix B.) Teachers may decide on the scope of the project's topic. You can choose whether the project will touch on all categories mentioned in the web or whether the focus will be only on certain aspects.

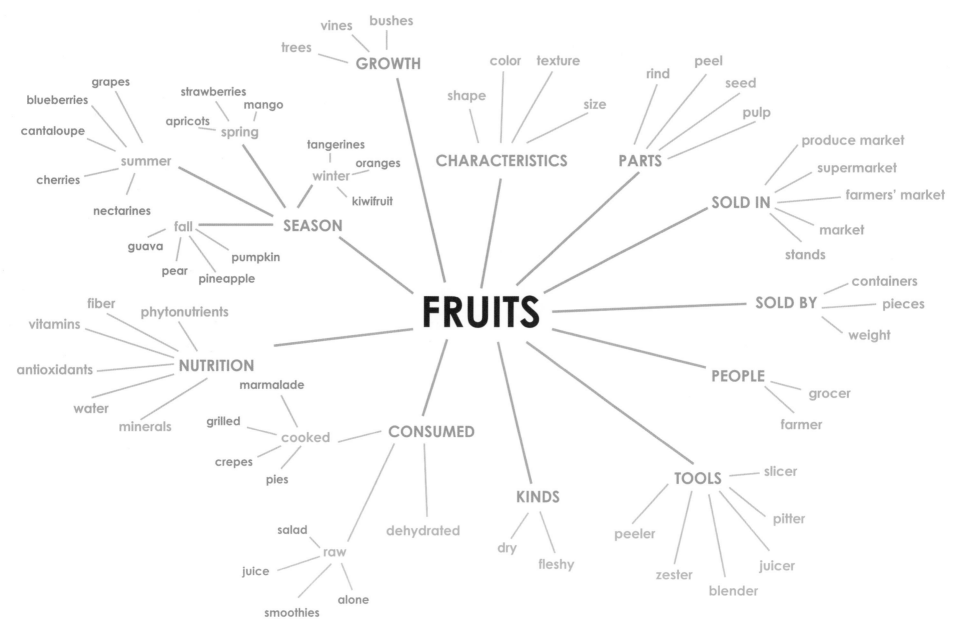

When you have completed the web, it is helpful to do a second web that organizes ideas in relation to areas of the curriculum, learning standards, and potential learning experiences.

Scientific Thinking
- Recognizes changes in the appearance, behavior, and habitats of living things
- Describes characteristics of plants, animals, and people
- Explores and describes similarities, differences, and categories of plants and animals
- Asks questions about growth and change in plants and animals

Scientific Thinking
- Uses all five senses to examine objects in detail
- Identifies similarities or differences between objects
- Explores natural phenomena through the senses
- Uses standard tools to explore the environment

Scientific Thinking
Communicates information learned from exploring the natural world

Literacy and Social Studies
- Retells a simple story or event in roughly sequential order
- Begins to understand concepts and language of geography related to home, school, and community
- Demonstrates awareness that money is needed to purchase goods and services

Scientific Thinking and Language
- Collects information about the natural world
- Recognizes changes in the appearance, behavior, and habitats of living things
- Describes simple relationships among plants, animals, and the environment
- Uses common vocabulary to discuss changes in the weather and seasons

Mathematics and Language
- Explores and develops vocabulary for length and weight
- Uses some vocabulary of measurement, but may not understand exact meanings of the words

Physical Well-Being and Health
- Participates in preparing nutritious foods
- Chooses nutritious foods rather than less-nutritious foods, with assistance
- Recognizes foods from different food groups, with assistance

Scientific Thinking and Language
- Participates in experiments, with assistance, and describes observations
- Makes predictions and develops generalizations based on past experiences
- Uses vocabulary that shows some recognition of scientific principles to explain why things happen
- Records information from an experience

Mathematics and Numeracy
- Identifies categories of objects
- Sorts objects into categories, classifying and comparing by characteristics
- Counts the number of objects in a group
- Orders objects by size, weight, height, length, and volume, with assistance

Social Studies
- Recognizes that people have different roles and jobs in the community
- Recognizes that people rely on others for goods and services
- Pretends to be different community members during play

Social Studies
- Identifies some ways technology helps people accomplish tasks
- Identifies ways of doing tasks both with and without technology

FRUITS

GROWTH
CHARACTERISTICS
PARTS
SOLD IN
SEASON
SOLD BY
NUTRITION
PEOPLE
CONSUMED
TOOLS
KINDS

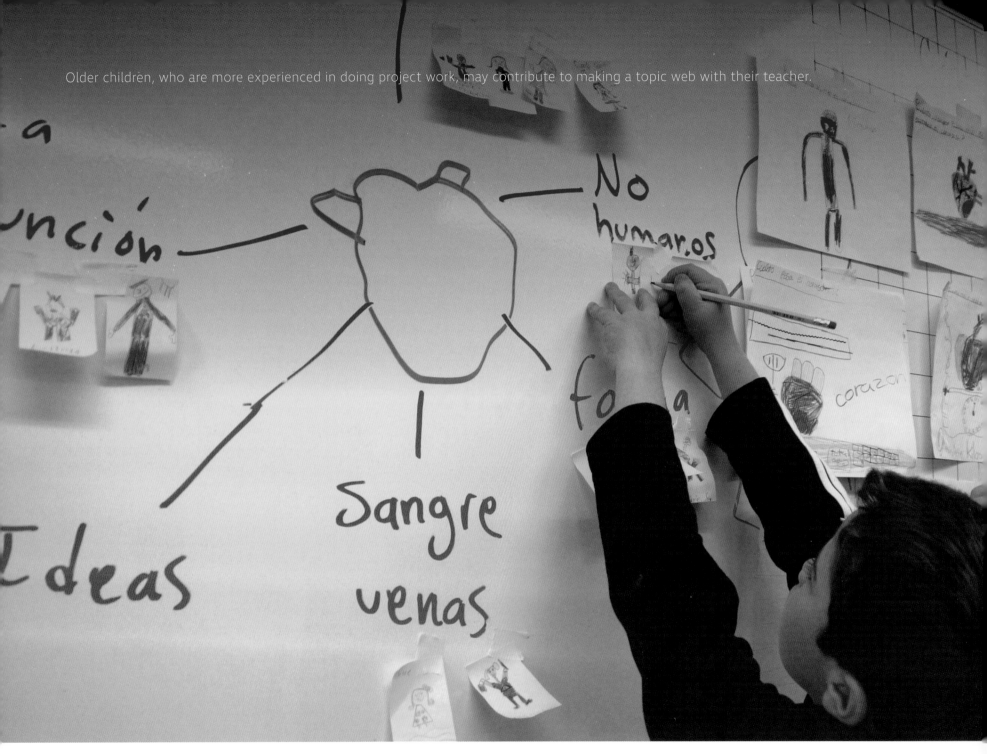

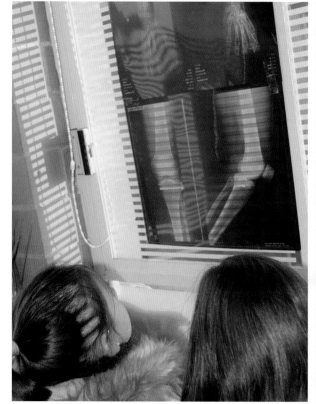

Engaging the Children's Interest

To introduce the topic of study, you may plan a provocation to spark the children's interest. At times, a teacher can choose to invite children to interact with certain familiar objects, or he can bring a picture and tell a personal story that could prompt a discussion. Telling stories, showing objects, or using another strategy to provoke wondering should not be exotic or overexciting; it should be quite common and close to the children's lives. The goal is to initiate conversations about personal experiences, ideas, and information about the topic that children can share and exchange with their classmates and that can reveal any misconceptions. This initial work is important for teachers, as it helps build a common basic understanding from which to begin to plan experiences for the investigation of the topic.

Expressing Initial Understanding and Knowledge

Throughout the course of a week or more, children may express their prior knowledge, current understanding, and personal stories about a topic in different ways. Your role as the teacher is to offer and support a variety of representational strategies through which children can best communicate and share their experiences. They could do this orally, through dramatic play, by drawing or painting, through writing, or by making models. These initial representations will not be very accurate or detailed, because the investigation has not commenced and the children do not yet have in-depth knowledge of the topic.

"I was going down to my garden on the elevator and I saw a bird falling from a nest."
Emi

"We like going to McDonald's, but my dad always orders take-out, we never eat there." Isabella

Wan dei aftr brlet clas my sistr tuec hr tutu off and shi pet it on top of a lamp. Then wi went to get diner and it sarted smeling like sonfing was burnig and my mom fand the tutu on fair. Nau my sistr nous shi shud not du that.

Family members can be valuable contributors to the development of a project. In this first phase, they may send objects to school that are related to the project. They can also share memories of events, through stories and photographs of experiences their children have had. These contributions can enrich class conversations. It is helpful to send families a letter introducing the topic their children will be studying during the course of several weeks. (For an example of a letter to send home, see appendix C.)

Rocks from aunt Pichi's house

Rocks from Valle de Bravo

The teacher can help the children share their experiences by displaying their work on classroom walls, tables, or shelves. These displays can enrich discussions about the topic and share the representational techniques children use. From the beginning of a project, you may also want to display photographs children bring from home or photographs of episodes of dramatic play that take place in the classroom. You can also display objects and models. You can group the items into categories, and you can write labels and explanatory captions for the different items.

Alonso brought pictures of himself and his family on a fishing boat.

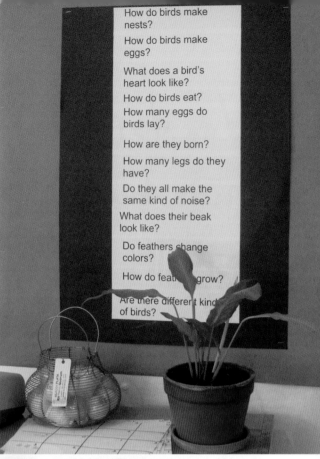

How do birds make nests?

How do birds make eggs?

What does a bird's heart look like?

How do birds eat?

How many eggs do birds lay?

How are they born?

How many legs do they have?

Do they all make the same kind of noise?

What does their beak look like?

Do feathers change colors?

How do feathers grow?

Are there different kinds of birds?

Identifying and Formulating Questions for the Investigation

As conversations about the topic and interaction with objects are taking place, children's wonderings often arise, and excitement and curiosity are expressed in the classroom. You may start noting what children want to learn more about and which personal interests they may want to pursue through the investigation. Teachers of toddlers may examine the children's interactions with repeated or different provocations to identify their questions and interests, which can be the foundation for the investigation.

Exploring Sounds

To provoke the children's interest on the topic of sounds, a teacher of toddlers set out different drum-like and stick-like objects on a table and invited the children to interact with them. She documented some of the children's comments and actions. A child banging with a straw on a metallic can said, "This doesn't work!" Another child said, "Mine is loud." Other children started making similar comments about the kinds of sounds being produced by the materials with which they interacted. After analyzing the documentation of this experience, the teacher identified the following questions for the children's research:

• How can you make different sounds?

• What kinds of sounds do different objects make?

Preschoolers and students in early elementary grades may express their wonderings as toddlers do. After having the opportunity to connect with their prior knowledge, they are also able—with the guidance of their teacher—to formulate questions for investigation. These questions may be collected during the course of several days or even a couple of weeks. It may be helpful for you to use a large piece of chart paper that you can post on your classroom wall while you write the questions that children may want to investigate.

Questions about Butterflies

- How do butterflies turn into butterflies?

- Do butterflies have bones?

- Do butterflies sleep?

- Where do butterflies live?

- What do butterflies eat?

- Do butterflies have a family?

Teachers often feel an impulse to give information to children right away, but hold it! Children benefit most when they can think about the questions themselves, formulate hypotheses, and look for ways to find the answers. You may scaffold their predictions to elicit the extent of their knowledge by asking questions such as, "What makes you say so?" or "How do you think it works?" Children will have differences of opinion about how objects or places function and about what people do. These controversies can arouse high levels of interest in finding answers to their questions. Some teachers like to record and make visible for their students the questions they formulate, the predictions they make, their findings, and how they discover the information. (For an example of this type of record for a project on fruit, see appendix D.)

Once the children's questions emerge by the end of phase 1, it is time for you to consider what children want to find out, what they want to look at more closely, whom to invite as a visiting expert, and where to go on a field trip to gather information. By the end of this phase, teachers are ready to plan experiences that will support children's research and help them seek answers to their questions.

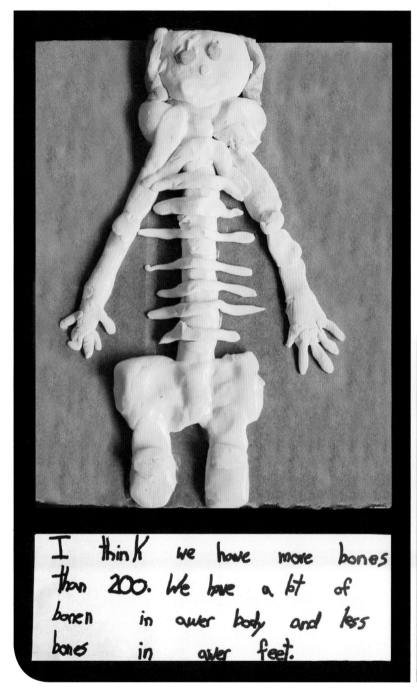

I think we have more bones than 200. We have a lot of bonen in awer body and less bones in awer feet.

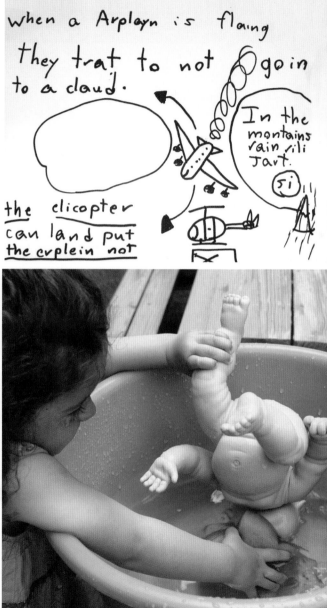

when a Arplayn is flaing they trat to not goin to a claud.

In the montains rain rili Jart.

si

the elicopter can land put the crplein not

4

Developing the Project

In phase 2, you will focus on how to help children find answers to their questions and represent their understanding. This phase of the project positions students as observers, investigators, reflective thinkers, and collaborators. They build on past experiences as they interact with their environment, visit field sites, and speak with experts. Through these experiences, children construct knowledge. Children use their understanding and skills to represent what they learn.

Phase 2 involves the following opportunities for learning:

- The teacher arranges for children to conduct fieldwork and talk to experts.

- Students are involved in firsthand learning and exploration.

- Children seek answers to the questions raised in phase 1 and think of new questions.

- The teacher provides additional sources for research.

- Children use various materials and representational strategies to show their understanding.

- The teacher displays experiences and work processes showing aspects of the investigation that children may discuss and revisit.

Choosing a Field Site

Good places for field trips usually include small establishments or places where children may get firsthand information that will help them answer their questions and bring evidence and new knowledge back to the classroom. It is a good idea to make a preliminary visit to evaluate the field site and to meet with the people in charge, so that you may discuss some of the children's questions and suitable procedures for moving the children through the location.

Items to Observe

While at the field site, children may see some of the following:

- Equipment
- Vehicles
- Machinery
- Tools needed to do a job
- People at work
- Clothing and gear used for different jobs

- Events
- Processes
- Recording and measuring devices
- Plants
- Animals
- Physical spaces

Field trips for toddlers may take place in the school itself or in its vicinity, because it is challenging to transport them and take all the necessary precautions to care for them.

Older students can go on longer trips, but it is important for teachers to consider the distance to the field site. The children might get hungry, grow tired, or need to use the bathroom during long bus rides.

During a field trip, children can record sights, sounds, smells, and textures. It is important for them to have means of recording their observations. They can take notes, record the textures of objects, collect samples, measure objects, ask questions, and take photographs.

Tools and Materials

Teachers may use some of the following tools and materials to record information at a field site:

- A clipboard and pencil to make field sketches and take notes

- Crayons to record textures by doing rubbings

- A magnifying glass to take a closer look at objects

- A camera or video recorder to capture images

- A measuring tape or items that can serve as nonstandard units of measurement to calculate the length and width of objects

- A small bag to collect samples

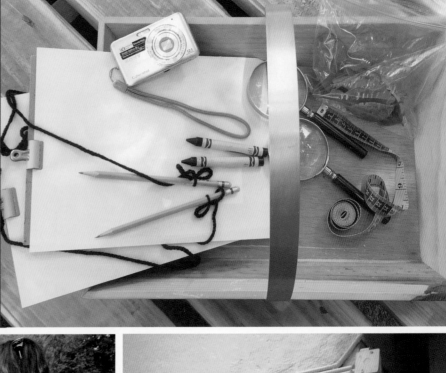

When you invite family members to join you on field trips, it can be valuable to meet with them before the visit to give them instructions about how to help the children carry out activities and document the experience. (To see an example of written instructions teachers may give to family members in preparation for a field trip, see appendices E and F.)

Children often remember recent events vividly and with much detail. After returning from a field trip, you may lead a discussion the same day or the following one to help youngsters review the visit. You may show photographs or video taken at the site to help youngsters revisit the experience and re-create it in their minds. You may also invite children to organize photographs, following the events in the order they happened. Even some toddlers are able to arrange photographs of the visit in a sequence, especially when the teacher selects very few photos.

If children collect objects at the field site, they may want to compare their collections with those of their peers and organize them by different attributes. Children may also share their field notes and look at samples of objects, if any were collected at the site. You may also invite students to share their field sketches with their classmates and talk about what they have drawn. This may be helpful, as they could be reminded of things that caught their attention.

At this point, you and the children may review the original list of questions, compare it with children's predictions, and determine which questions were answered at the site and which remain to be investigated. Project work provides many examples of how answers to questions often lead to more questions, so any new queries inspired by the visit can be added to the original list. This post-visit work may also help you identify the children's interests and set the tone for the work to follow. You may also want to bring in books, explore Internet sites, and use any other resources that provide additional information.

Regina said, "The doctor told us that we need to get vaccines so we won't get sick."

Inviting Experts to Visit

At times and for a number of reasons, it may be challenging for teachers to take their class to a field site. However, teachers can invite experts to the school to contribute valuable information that can enrich the study of a topic. An expert could be anyone who knows more about the topic than the children do. It could be a parent, a local expert, or even a person who works at the school. You could use digital media to communicate and work collaboratively with an expert at a distance. You can often find more people willing to talk with children than you would imagine.

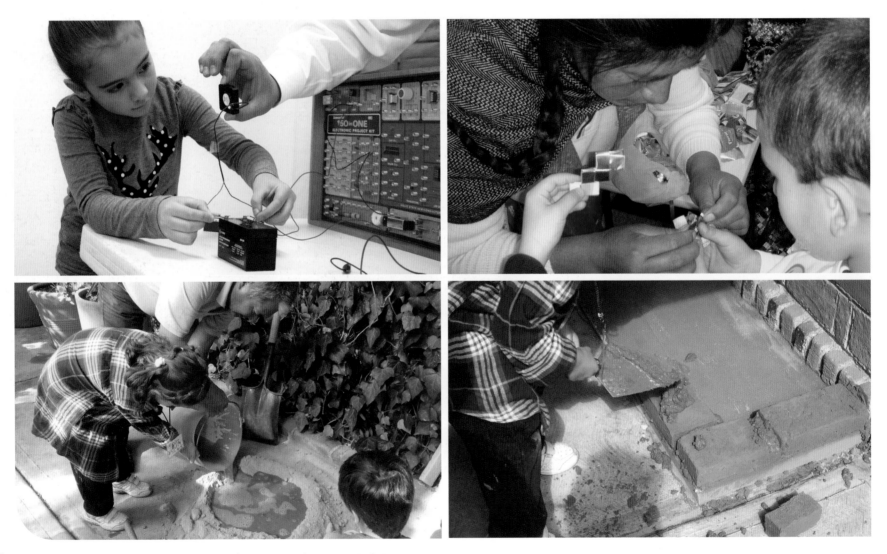

Children Expressing Ideas and Representing Understanding

As the study of a topic progresses and the children begin to find answers to some of their questions, they set out to represent what they have learned. The class is usually divided into several smaller groups who share similar interests in different aspects of the topic.

In a project on fruit, for example, some children might be interested in different kinds of fruit. A second group might focus on how fruit is consumed, and another group might study where fruit is sold.

Grouping children, rather than having them work individually, can build a sense of community in the classroom and can offer opportunities for youngsters and adults to learn together and from each other. Older children are usually more experienced at working together with some guidance. However, younger children may also benefit from cooperating with each other to reach a common goal, as it promotes the development of their growing social and emotional competencies.

Toddlers are still at an egocentric stage of emotional development. Although some toddlers might begin to notice and show interest in what their peers are doing, others might not. When encouraged to create something together, they usually work in parallel. They might be physically side by side or in front of each other, but they are working in their own spaces rather than doing something together. This arrangement does not diminish the value of this shared experience because it lays important foundations for collaborative work.

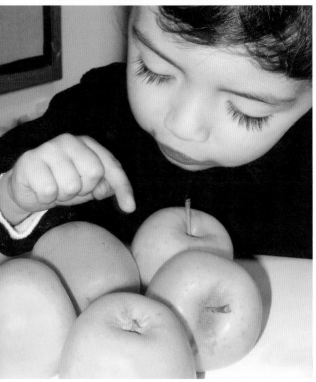

Exploring Tools and Materials for Representing Knowledge

Children of different ages can employ quite a range of representational strategies and techniques. Toddlers require ample time to simply explore tools and materials, such as clay, paint, paintbrushes, markers, glue, and scissors. It is helpful if they can do this before learning representational strategies. Some teachers may hesitate to encourage young children to use different materials, as they might be concerned about safety or about the appearance of the classroom. However, when young children are guided in how to use these tools and materials, they are usually quite able and willing to follow the required procedures. It works well to provide a variety of materials and let the child choose, with your guidance, which one to use for a particular representation.

Representations may vary widely in diversity and complexity, depending on the child's level of maturity and ability to use the materials, tools, and representational strategies. Some forms of representation might be adequate for young children, while others might be best used when children are older.

Toddlers and preschoolers may best express their understanding by constructing with blocks or other materials, engaging in dramatic play, making models, and creating drawings and paintings. Some of the more mature preschoolers and early elementary children might be able to make maps, diagrams, charts, graphs, dichotomies, and timelines and might express their understanding through pieces of writing and by putting together presentations using digital media.

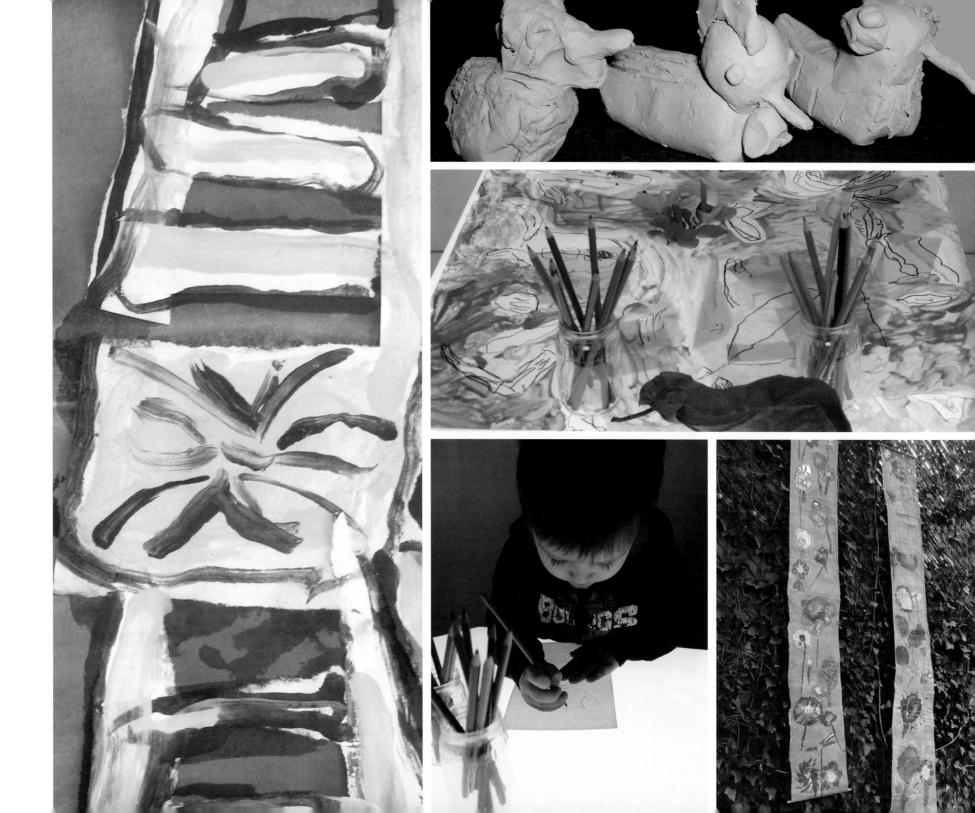

The older the children, the more interested they will be in accuracy and in getting their representations to correspond in satisfying ways with the real world they are learning about. It is important to remember that the products of representation do not need to be visually beautiful; their beauty and value lie in the process behind them and the understanding they reflect.

Naturally, children learn most about explorations in which they are directly involved. But they also learn a great deal from work done by classmates because it shows them other aspects of the topic being studied, other representational strategies and materials used, and the challenges their peers encountered in making their representations.

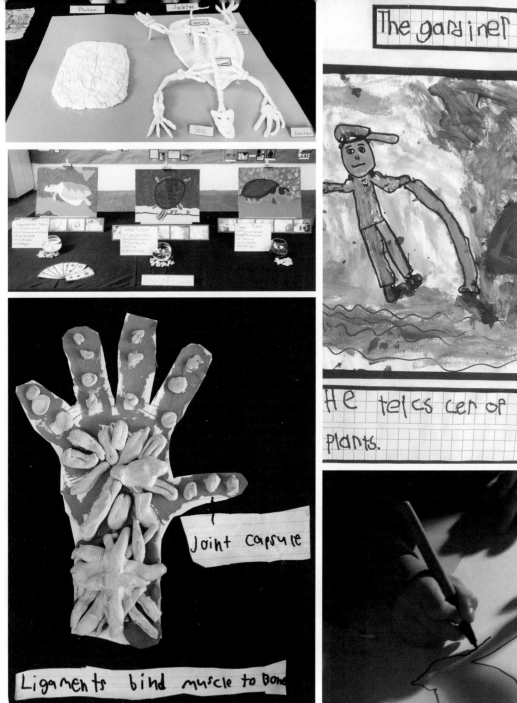

What does our body do with the food we eat?

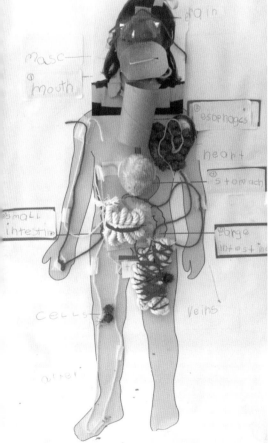

brain

masc
mouth

esophagus

heart

stomach

small intestine

large intestine

cells

veins

WINDOS

DOR

TAYERS

HOBCAP

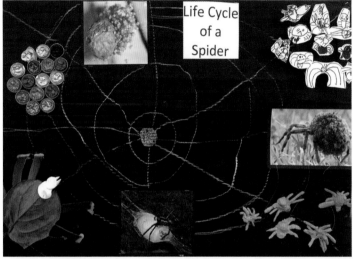

Life Cycle of a Spider

BlaC KeiP BeRd

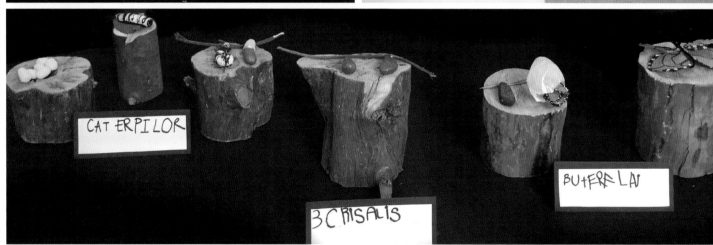

CATERPILOR

3 CRISALIS

BUTERRLAI

The duration of the process of representation may vary greatly; however, it usually involves the largest portion of the project time. The time devoted to each session can also vary, but usually youngsters get engaged in the representation process and sometimes want to work for long periods of time. It is a good idea to consider planning for some uninterrupted, lengthy sessions. You may also want to consider arranging spaces in your classroom where you can store children's work—such as models or paintings—that will need to be revisited throughout several weeks. During the second phase of the project, the display on your classroom's walls may develop considerably. It may now reflect experiences during the field trip, the experts who have come to your classroom, the work processes being carried out, and the answers to some of the questions that the children formulated. When children are surrounded with informative and attractive work, they are drawn to examine it in detail. You may use a particular collection of work to conduct a discussion on one aspect of the topic, or you may encourage the children to look at specific wall displays that may help them in their developing representations. Displays of happenings and children's work encourage all members of the class to examine and evaluate the experiences they have had, the different techniques they have used, and the ways in which they have solved problems.

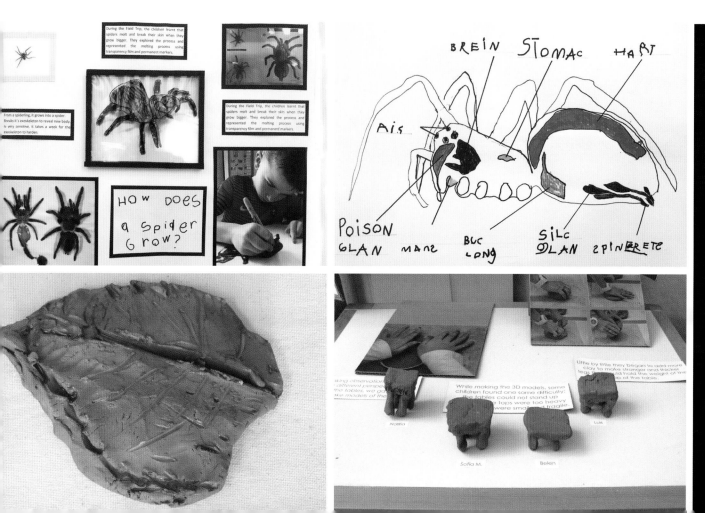

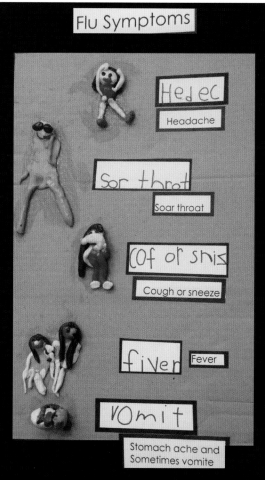

5

Bringing the Project to a Close

In phase 3, you will focus on wrapping up the project and sharing the children's learning.

- The teacher decides when to conclude the project.

- With the guidance of their teacher, the children revisit and summarize the work done during the project.

- The teacher assesses how well the children have learned the main ideas that emerged from the study of a topic.

- The teacher, in consultation with the children, plans a culminating event to share the project work with members of the larger learning community.

After spending several weeks on phase 2, you will decide when and how to bring the project to a close. In making this decision, consider several factors: determine the children's interest in continuing or concluding the work, analyze whether the class members have answered most of their questions by conducting research and by representing their understanding in different ways, and take into account breaks in the school calendar that might help to naturally transition from one project to another.

43

This is a good time to review the story of the project through the documentation displayed on your classroom's walls and shelves, to revisit the events that took place, to identify the skills children used in the context of a project, and to examine the processes that led to the children's work products. The children may reflect on the work they accomplished individually as well as in a group. You may guide them in evaluating evidence of their progress during the project so they can appreciate their own growing competence and understanding.

Time one drawing of a bicycle

Time two drawing of a bicycl

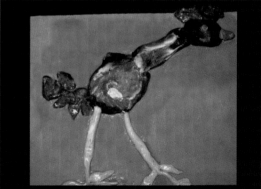

Teachers of young children usually decide how to conclude and share the project work. However, listen to your students' suggestions, because many times they show initiative and contribute great ideas for a culminating activity.

Young children are as eager and enthusiastic as older learners to share their work with family members, teachers, and peers. They demonstrate ownership and pride when they show pictures of themselves involved in exploration or products of their work. Most toddlers are able to point to their work and tell a story of their representations.

Every Child is an Artist
PICASSO

You have a wide variety of options for concluding a project. You may want to invite children from other classes, family members, or other visitors to see a display of the project documentation. This display could include photographs of children at work, narratives of stories to explain the progression of the project, and pieces of work made by the children. (For an example of an invitation to family members, see appendix G.)

Another option would be to put together a digital presentation that includes photographs and videos of events and processes that engaged the children during the study of the topic.

Many teachers choose to keep a collection of work to make a class book or to place each child's work in a folder that they can take home and share with their families.

Others might prefer to plan a culminating event that highlights children's experiences during the project and the knowledge they gained. For example, a teacher and her students set up a restaurant at school to show their understanding about how these kinds of establishments run, the different jobs people do, the uniforms they wear, and the equipment they use.

Some young children are not very talkative at home about what happens at school. Others might describe part of the project work in ways that family members have difficulty understanding. When families are given the opportunity to see the conclusion of a project, they become more knowledgeable about what their children do at school, and they feel grateful for having the opportunity to participate in their school life.

The third phase of a project is a time to reflect on and evaluate what has been learned. It is also a good time to look forward to exploring fresh ideas and applying skills in the study of a new topic.

6 Supporting Social and Emotional Development during a Project

Educational programs often emphasize cognitive development and academic standards with measurable outcomes, yet social and emotional development require serious attention as well.

Studies of the mind strongly suggest that children may benefit from developing social-emotional competencies such as regulating their emotions, solving problems, making choices, persisting to accomplish what they set out to do, and working collaboratively. These executive skills will enable children to set goals and achieve them; to lay the foundations for building healthy relationships and interactions at home, at school, and in the larger community; and to promote the acquisition of knowledge and cognitive skills. (For detailed examples of how project work can enhance social-emotional development, see appendix H.)

Through project work, children develop social and emotional competencies while being intellectually engaged and making genuine choices. A child's disposition to work in a classroom is strengthened by a sense of purpose, which projects can support. Children can assume some of the responsibility for the kinds of work they undertake, and the teacher can promote conditions that allow students to accomplish what they set out to do.

In contrast with systematic instruction, the teacher does not assess his students in terms of meeting requirements or achieving predetermined skills and understandings. In project work, the teacher looks at the children from a different perspective. He sees them in terms of their individual strengths, what they can already do and feel confident with, and how they might use their capabilities. Consequently, children can rely on the expertise of the teacher or other adults for guidance as they take responsibility for engaging in project-related tasks. During this process, children feel a sense of accomplishment that can strengthen their self-esteem and encourage them to strive to realize their personal goals. Teachers who have worked with the project approach say that children frequently gain satisfaction from hard work, cooperative efforts, and overcoming obstacles that might arise.

Picturing the Project Approach | Creative Explorations in Early Learning

Another aim of the project approach is to enable children to experience the class as a community, where everyone is encouraged and expected to contribute to the learning of the whole group in different ways.

Children Working Collaboratively with Peers

Collaborative work encourages children to ask questions, plan together, use their strengths, discuss challenges, make things, solve problems, negotiate solutions, and share their work. When children share their stories of experience, they become curious about what they share and what is distinctive about their own experience with a topic. As children listen to one another and work together, they take increasing interest in the questions and wonderings of their peers. They can then partner or group themselves with other classmates to conduct research, find answers to their questions together, and engage in representations that will reflect what they have learned.

Children Working Collaboratively with Adults

Adults who play the role of experts are vital in the development of a project. They provide firsthand information about the topic the children are investigating. The staff members at the field site usually share their expertise with the young visitors. Children who have particular interests can ask questions, and everyone in the group can benefit from the answers given by the experts. Children tend to feel great satisfaction when sharing their expertise with other people. By observing, listening, and talking to youngsters, adults can gain valuable insight into how children think, how they understand things, and how they work.

Your role as a teacher is vital in supporting the children's feelings of belonging to a group, where individuals may contribute their skills, knowledge, and insights for the collective learning experience to reach goals that would be difficult to achieve individually.

7 Promoting STEM Learning during a Project

Legislators and educators are recognizing the importance of science, technology, engineering, and mathematics (STEM) education for success in the workforce and for solving the complex problems that communities and nations will face in the future. The project approach and its framework can naturally facilitate and promote the development of STEM skills in preschoolers and early elementary students.

The type of learning that is seen with the project approach and in STEM-oriented classrooms differs considerably from the preplanned lessons of a published curriculum. Although project work supports the curriculum standards identified for testing in the different subject areas, teachers do not teach to the test through project work nor through the integrated STEM approach. The emphasis is on the context in which learning is intrinsically motivating and engaging to young children because of its focus on real-world application of knowledge and skill.

STEM goals and the project approach support learning in the following similar ways:

- Both focus on students' active learning.

- They support the idea that learning is maximized when children can build on their prior knowledge to construct new understandings relevant to the real world.

- They promote children's abilities to formulate questions, make predictions, and conduct research to collect data.

- Both provide students with opportunities to work both individually and collaboratively.

- They encourage children to follow their interests and show initiative in the study of a topic or the solving of a problem.

- They foster experiences that provide interdisciplinary learning.

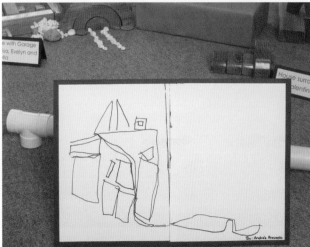

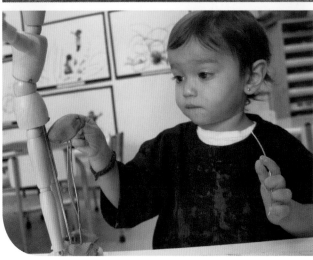

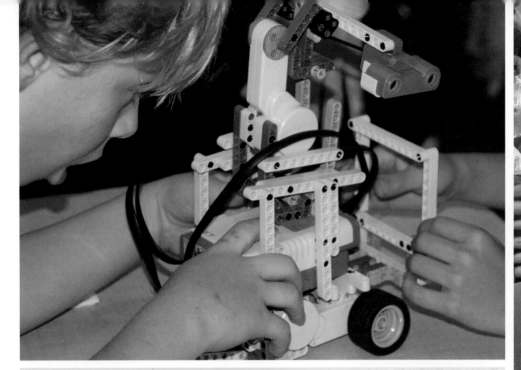

STEM education encourages children to ask questions and craft solutions to problems they identify. They investigate and reflect on what they learn. The project approach involves those same skills and can support children's efforts to follow their interests and acquire STEM competencies through meaningful experiences and interactions with people and the environment. Experience with this type of approach will serve children's critical-thinking and problem-solving capabilities now and later in life. (See appendix I for more ways that project work supports STEM objectives.)

8

Sharing Project Stories

In this section, you will find stories of projects that took place at a school in Mexico City, Mexico. This institution implemented the project approach with children ages two to six more than fifteen years ago. Some years later, the school also implemented this approach throughout the elementary grades. Parents whose children attend this school often comment that project work makes it unique and that it is a strong reason they have chosen the school for their children. Moreover, teachers seeking employment are drawn to apply to this institution because of their interest in project work.

A Home for Fish: The Fish Tank Project

- A project by two- and three-year-old children

- Duration of the project: ten weeks

Phase 1—Beginning the Project

The toddlers in Ms. Karen's class enjoyed looking at the books she had in the bookshelf; among them were a couple of books about fish. She often observed that children seemed interested in fish, and she began listening more closely to conversations some children were having about this topic. A couple of children had fish as pets in their homes and shared their knowledge with their peers. Ms. Karen noticed that the interest in fish persisted among many children in the class throughout the course of several weeks, and she decided to select the topic of pet fish as the subject of an in-depth study.

She then applied herself to developing a project planning web of ideas to envision the potential of this topic.

To provoke the interest of all the children in her class, Ms. Karen brought in an empty fish tank and placed it on a shelf where everyone could see it. Almost immediately, several children noticed this new object in their classroom. Some pointed at the tank; others approached it, took a look, and began having conversations about it with others. Over the course of several days, the teacher documented what some children said.

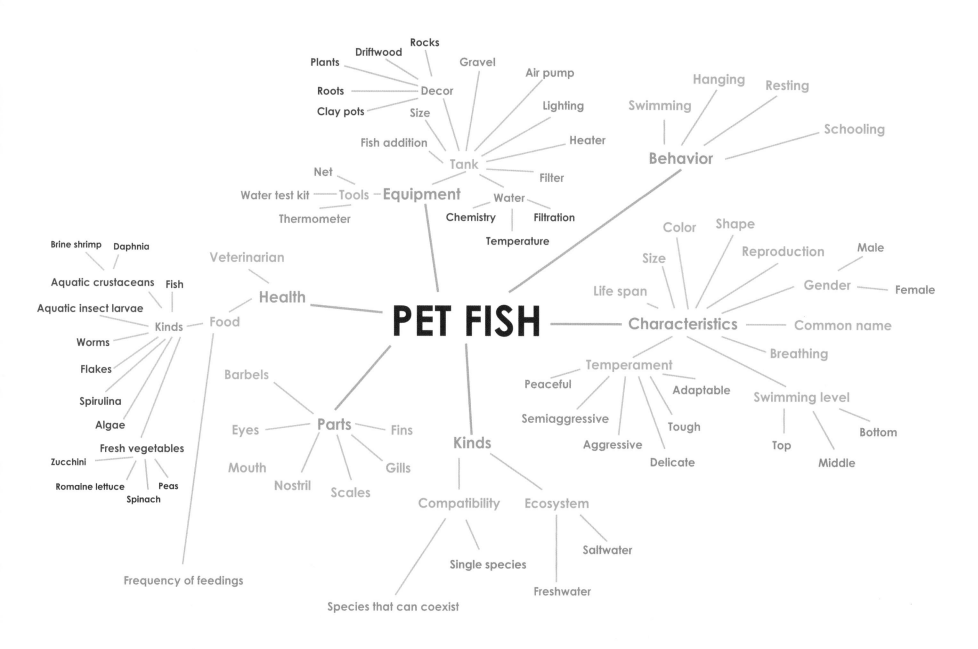

"What is that thing?" "It's a fish box." "A very big box." "A house for fish." "It needs a bed for the fish to sleep, then they will wake up and dance and sing." "Fish swim in the water." "They have a mouth, a nose, and wings." "We will need to get them food to eat; they can eat pizza." "And lettuce and an apple." "The house needs water." "They need the sun and a lot of water." "The house needs a roof."

After analyzing the children's comments and conversations, the teacher identified several questions for research:

- What things are needed to set up a fish tank, and what are they for?

- What do pet fish eat?

- What are the body parts of fish?

To continue assessing the youngsters' previous knowledge, the teacher invited her students to make some initial drawings from memory.

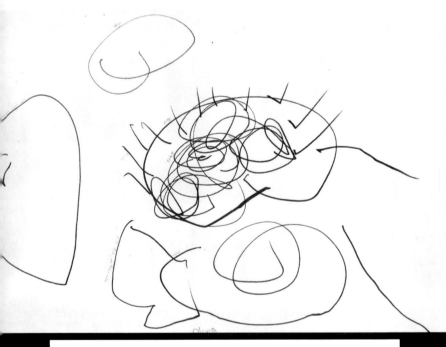

A big fish with many eyes and hands. Two small fish. They swim in the water. This is their watery house.

This is Acapulco, and these are fish. When I moved the fish ran away. This is water and a bedroom of the fish for sleeping. There is a lamp too. - Valentina

Some children drew their hypotheses of things they thought should be placed inside a fish tank. They predicted that the empty tank needed a light; a kitchen; a room with a bed, a blanket, and a painting; a bathroom; food; a supermarket to get food; flowers; toys; and water.

Phase 2—Developing the Project

Ms. Karen was now ready to plan learning experiences for the children to find the answers to their questions. For safety reasons and logistics, toddlers at this school don't usually go on field trips. Teachers often rely on experts and digital media so that children can get information, as was the case in this situation.

First, Ms. Karen projected digital images of fish—to help children note the characteristics of different types—and images of fish tanks that had already been set up. While looking at the images projected on the wall, children held conversations and took notes.

After this experience, Ms. Karen invited a group of children to work collaboratively using an electronic tablet to create a digital representation of the elements needed to set up a fish tank.

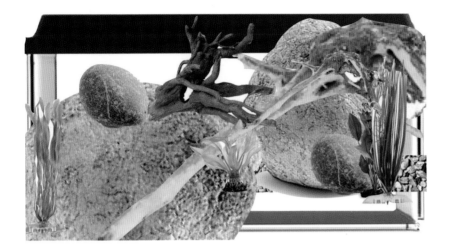

The children in this small group shared their digital representation with the class. It showed a fish tank that included natural elements such as rocks, sticks, and plants.

Next, Ms. Karen invited an expert to come in and help students set up a fish tank. He answered many of the children's questions about the elements that could be included in a fish tank, talked to them about which are essential to incorporate, and showed them how a tank is set up.

The children were absorbed in how he set up the fish tank, but it took them little time to discover that there were no fish in it.

To decide what kinds of fish they would buy for the tank, Ms. Karen invited children to bring in their pet fish for the class to observe.

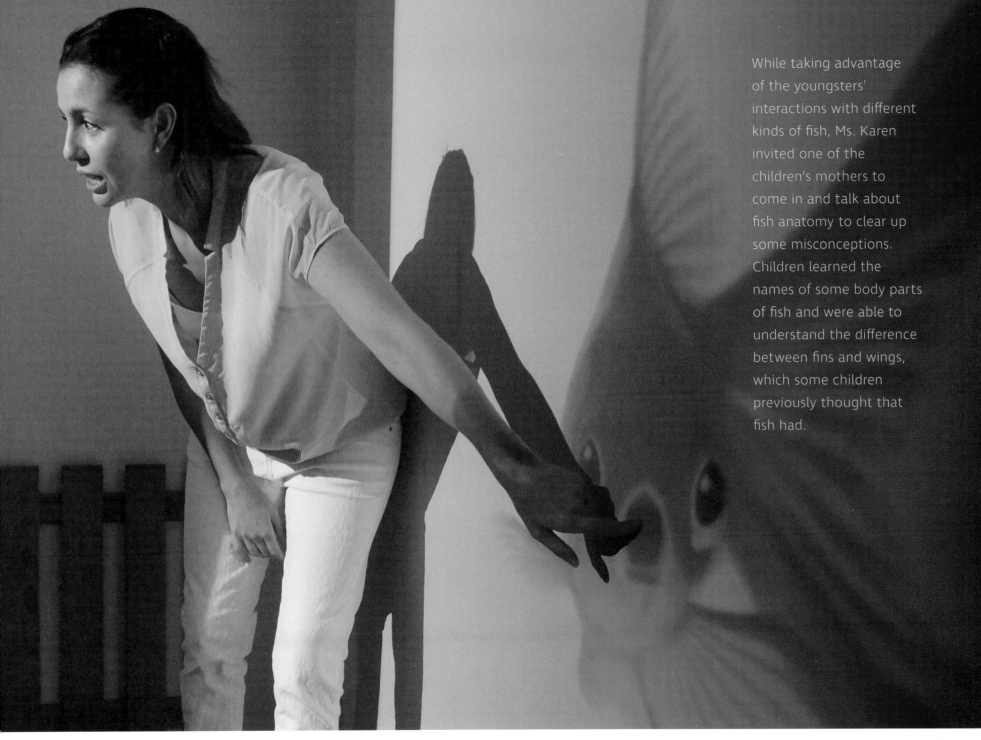

While taking advantage of the youngsters' interactions with different kinds of fish, Ms. Karen invited one of the children's mothers to come in and talk about fish anatomy to clear up some misconceptions. Children learned the names of some body parts of fish and were able to understand the difference between fins and wings, which some children previously thought that fish had.

Pedro, one of the children in the class, said, "I will bring the fish for the fish tank!"

A few days later, Pedro and his mom came into Ms. Karen's class with two goldfish inside plastic bags. Ms. Karen opened the bags so that the fish could swim into the tank. It was an eagerly awaited and significant moment for everyone in the class. Pedro and his mom also brought in fish food and tools to clean the tank.

The children learned how much and how many times per day the fish should eat. The teacher created a calendar so that everyone would get a chance to feed them.

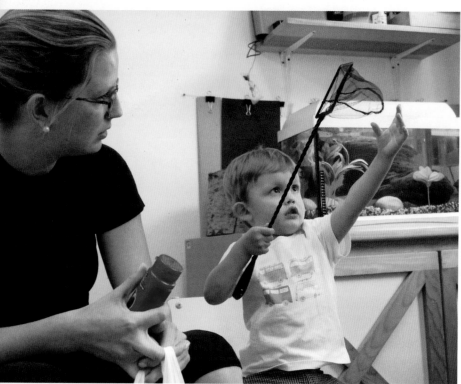

Phase 3—Concluding the Project

After many weeks of exploration, Ms. Karen decided that even though new questions were still arising, the children had answered the original questions they had set out to research and that it was now time to conclude the project.

She took time to analyze the children's initial representations of fish and to assess how their understanding had evolved throughout the course of the project.

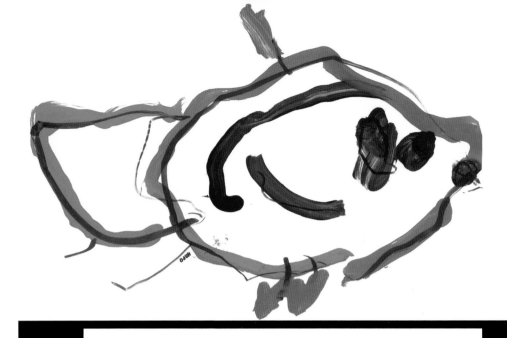

Hugo's time two drawing from memory.

Hugo's time one drawing from memory.

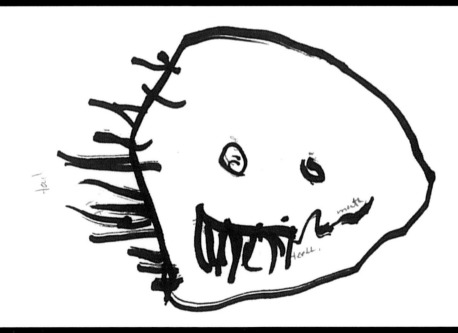

Hugo's obsevational drawing of a fish.

Ms. Karen also decided to plan a culminating event to share the project. She wanted visitors to have the sensation that they were walking inside a fish tank. Ms. Karen and her students turned the classroom into a huge replica of the fish tank that they had put together throughout the course of the project. The children made fish out of discarded plastic containers and pieces of fabric. They also represented plants and rocks with paintings and models.

The day of the culminating event, Ms. Karen shared a digital presentation with parents, which highlighted the learning experiences that her students had had during the project. Finally, the children walked into the simulated fish tank with their parents and proudly shared the images, processes, and products of their work.

The Car Project

- A project by three- and four-year-old children

- A collaborative experience between two teachers of different classes conducting a study on the same topic.

- Duration of the project: eight weeks

Phase 1—Beginning the Project

Ms. Rose and Ms. Mar, two teachers of the same grade level, decided that it would be an interesting experience to study a topic as a collaborative experience that would involve children and parents from two different classes. They also thought it would be an opportunity for them to learn together and from each other. They held a conversation about which topic could be relevant and meaningful for the children to study. After thinking about several, they decided that conducting a study of cars could be a good possibility, since most of them travel by car each day. The teachers made a topic web to envision the many possibilities that the children might research. They decided to do this planning before the vacation period, as they thought it would be a good idea to get organized; collect items and other resources they could use; and reflect on the opportunities for investigation, representation, and the application of skills that this topic might provide for the children.

After the winter break, Ms. Mar told her class about the car trip she had taken over the holidays. She showed them photographs and told the children about the distances she had traveled, the different kinds of roads and highways she had traveled on, and even about the car trouble she had faced. Next, she visited Ms. Rose's class and gave the same presentation.

The two teachers mixed the youngsters from their classes, organized them in small groups, and invited them to share stories about cars. Most of the children participated eagerly and had a lot to share about this topic. Some of their stories related to the types, sizes, colors, and parts of cars. Other children talked about accidents, cars breaking down and how they are fixed, and where their families go when traveling by car.

This is me in the car with my mom. She uses her seatbelt and help me wear mine.

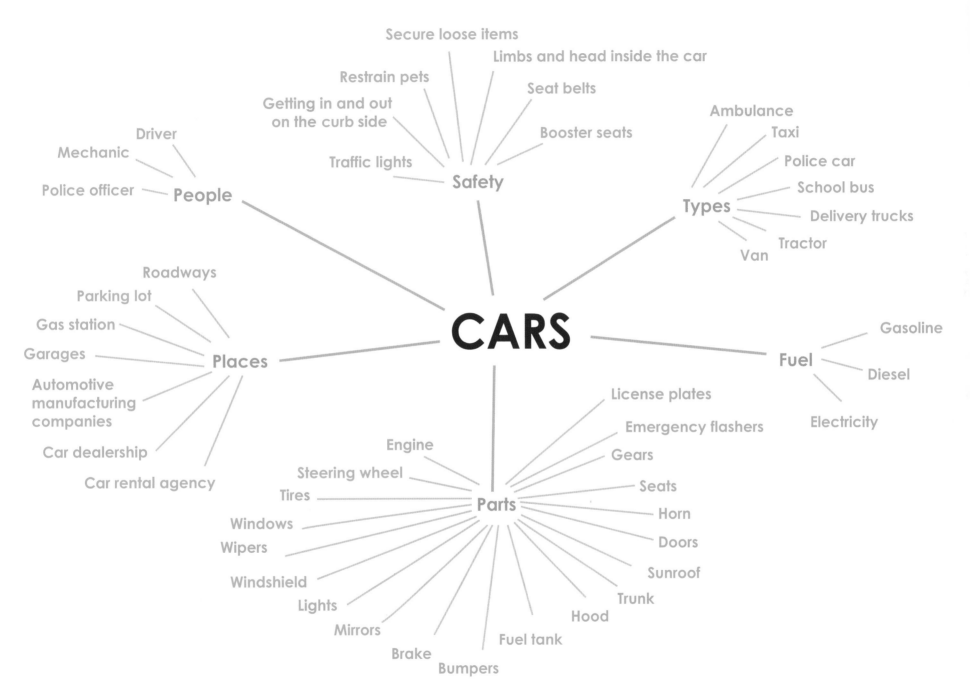

CARS

Safety
- Secure loose items
- Limbs and head inside the car
- Seat belts
- Restrain pets
- Booster seats
- Getting in and out on the curb side
- Traffic lights

People
- Driver
- Mechanic
- Police officer

Types
- Ambulance
- Taxi
- Police car
- School bus
- Delivery trucks
- Tractor
- Van

Places
- Roadways
- Parking lot
- Gas station
- Garages
- Automotive manufacturing companies
- Car dealership
- Car rental agency

Fuel
- Gasoline
- Diesel
- Electricity

Parts
- Engine
- Steering wheel
- Tires
- Windows
- Wipers
- Windshield
- Lights
- Mirrors
- Brake
- Bumpers
- Fuel tank
- Hood
- Trunk
- Sunroof
- Doors
- Horn
- Seats
- Gears
- Emergency flashers
- License plates

Together, Ms. Mar and Ms. Rose looked at the documentation of the children's conversations and drawings and identified the initial questions that their students showed interest in learning more about.

- What are the different parts of cars?

- How are cars fixed?

- How are cars built?

The teachers informed families about the joint venture their classes would undertake and asked for their possible contributions. They asked whether family members could talk to the children as experts, share materials, or offer to make arrangements for possible field trips.

Phase 2—Developing the Project

Ms. Rose and Ms. Mar identified some of the aspects of the topic that most of the children in their classes were interested in learning about and grouped their students accordingly.

What are the different parts of cars?

By listening to the conversations of the children in this group, the teachers could see that a few children knew some of the specialized vocabulary for the parts of cars, but that many others didn't. They also noticed that the children did not mention many components of cars at all.

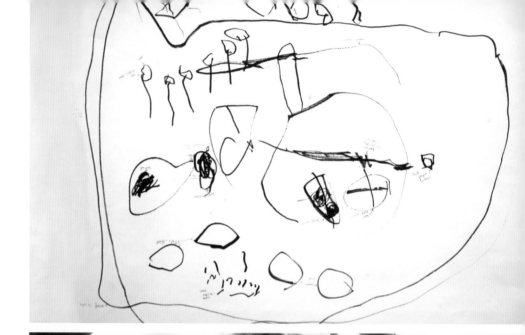

- "A car has doors and seats."

- "It has sticks that move when it rains."

- "Cars have a hole in the back. My mom uses it to put the things we buy at the supermarket."

- "Cars have horns that sound beep, beep."

While holding this conversation, the children made a collaborative drawing from memory showing the parts of a car.

Ms. Mar and Ms. Rose invited an expert to speak to the class, and he brought his car to the school. The children were able to take a close look at it. The expert talked about the different parts of cars, the purposes they serve, and how they work.

This group of children documented their experience by taking pictures and recording a video. They made a digital dictionary to share with their peers the new specialized vocabulary they had learned about car parts.

How are cars fixed?

The youngsters interested in this aspect of the topic held many conversations about why cars break down, how they are fixed, who fixes them, and where they are repaired. They made predictions and represented their thoughts through drawings.

The teachers arranged a field trip to a garage, so children could clear up their misconceptions and have some of their questions answered.

When the children returned from the field trip, they found different car parts that the teachers had set out for them. Through dramatic play, the students represented the knowledge they had gained during the visit. They depicted processes they had seen, acted out roles of people they saw at work, and used new words in their play.

There are different doctors that fix the cars. They use medicines.

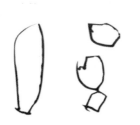

1. First the wheels go on so the car can go forward.

2. The windows, so there is air inside the car.

3. The steering wheel to make the car go forward.

4. The seats for people to sit.

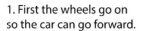

5. A seat for Mommy.

6. The engines.

7. Then we put everything together!

How are cars built?

The children in this group had all sorts of theories about this process. Discussions among them were quite lively and even a bit heated. Some agreed on what a few children suggested, while others strongly disagreed and formulated different hypotheses. In an attempt to reach agreement with their peers, three children made a graphic representation of how they thought cars were built.

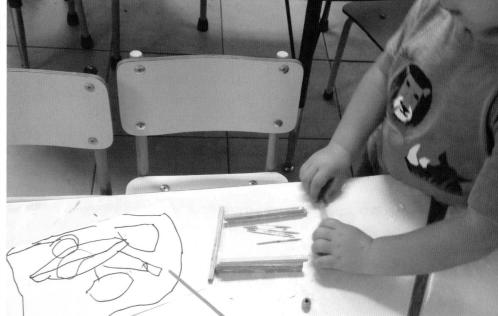

After their explanation, these children managed to convince a few others, but most still held to their different hypotheses. The teachers thought it would be a good moment to invite an expert on car manufacturing to their class. After all the discussion that had been going on, the students were eager to understand how this process really happened. The expert showed them a video and narrated every step of the process. He was surprised to hear many of the questions the children had, and he answered them most willingly.

One of the things that caught the interest of the children was the expert's explanation that cars are first designed and then built. To share this new knowledge with others, the children in this group went through the process of designing and making models of cars.

Phase 3—Concluding the Project

Ms. Mar and Ms. Rose had much to talk about and share with their colleagues, because this had been the first experience at the school that involved teachers and children from two classes working together on the same project. The two teachers commented that they felt enriched working this way, as they had had the opportunity to analyze, discuss, interpret, plan experiences, and assess the children's learning and the progress of the project together. They encouraged their colleagues to try this type of collaborative experience, which had helped them learn with and from each other.

As they had done throughout the project, the two teachers decided together when it was time to bring the project to a close. They invited families and other members of the school community to an exhibit that showcased the children's learning. Furthermore, this particular project display proved interesting for other teachers, as it featured the documentation of how this collaborative experience contributed to the professional growth of the two partner teachers.

The Garbage Project: Reducing, Reusing, and Recycling

- A project by six- and seven-year-old children

- Duration of the project: nine weeks

Phase 1—Beginning the Project

One of the units in the first-grade science curriculum requires children to learn about the environment, earth, and universe. Ms. Mory thought it would be useful for children to learn how trash affects the environment and the repercussions that the environmental effects have on their lives.

The teacher designed a topic web to explore the potential of a project on garbage.

To engage the children's interest in this topic, Ms. Mory brought to class a planter made out of a discarded polyethylene terephthalate (PET) container. She told a personal story of how she turned this plastic container she was going to throw away into a useful and beautiful object.

Some of the children in the class told stories of similar experiences, which they shared both orally with their classmates as well as through drawing and writing.

One day I ate siriol I saved the box and I made a cumura I used carton and toilet paper.

GARBAGE

Disposal
- Latex paint
- Turpentine
- Paint thinner
- Painting supplies
- Cleaning products
- Medicines
- Residential waste
- Human waste
- Pesticides
- Herbicides
- Tires
- Batteries

Hobby supplies
- Chemistry sets
- Resins
- Fiberglass
- Epoxy
- Glues
- Cements
- Wood preservatives
- Photographic chemicals
- Rubber-cement thinner

Collection
- Drop-off centers
- Buy-back centers
- Curbside collection

Impact
- Air
- Water
- Land

Recycle
- Symbols
- Centers
- Goods
  - Plastic
  - Electronics
  - Boxes
  - Paper
  - Compact fluorescent lights
  - Cans
  - Cardboard
  - Metal
  - Yard waste
  - Tetra Pak
  - Glass
- Save
  - Money
  - Natural resources
  - Energy

Reuse
- Containers
- Washable diapers
- Cloth napkins
- Cloth gift bags
- Sack shopping bags
- Secondhand
- Computers
- Books

Reduce
- Less packaging
- Bulk shopping
- Concentrates
- Durable goods
- Avoid junk mail
- Food garden
- Share
- Rent
- Donate

Next, Ms. Mory asked her students to bring items from home that they thought could be reused or recycled. During the next few days, the children brought all sorts of objects to class. They contributed items that are often thrown away, such as bottle caps, glass and plastic bottles, cans, and magazines. They also brought in old items that were no longer in use, such as keys, old pieces of jewelry, and silverware.

The children held discussions about how to organize the objects and decided to group them in different categories.

These first graders created a center in their classroom for reusing and recycling items and invited children from other classes to contribute objects.

After a few days of organizing objects and thinking about their properties and potential, the children formulated some questions for research:

• Why are there garbage containers of different colors at school, and what do the signs on them mean?

• What happens with all the trash that is produced at school?

• What is the difference between reusing and recycling?

• How can we use trash items to make things, and what things could we make with them?

Phase 2—Developing the Project

As Ms. Mory reflected on the questions that many of her students were interested in researching, she planned experiences that would help them find answers and gain new knowledge about the topic.

The first expert to visit was a member of the maintenance staff, who explained why the school has garbage cans of different colors and what each one is for. He taught children how to dispose of objects and showed them the large containers where all the garbage produced daily at school is stored. This group of children took field notes about the experience so they could share the information with their classmates.

Preliminary Ideas

Some children formulated hypotheses about their questions:

- "I think that to recycle plastic bottles, you leave them under the sun until they melt, and then you can use them again."

- "Recycling means to reuse things that you were going to throw away."

- "There are garbage cans of different colors to throw out different things."

A group of children made a time line to represent the information they learned from the expert.

To research the question about the difference between reusing and recycling, Ms. Mory arranged a field trip to a PET recycling plant.

The experts at the recycling plant explained that *recycling* means turning an item into raw materials, which may be used again, usually to make a completely different product. *Reusing*, on the other hand, refers to using an object without treatment to make something else.

Picturing the Project Approach | Creative Explorations in Early Learning

You throw PET bottles away.

The trash truck collects PET bottles and takes them to the recycling company.

They wash PET bottles in a machine.

Bottles are cut into small pieces.

A machine transforms the bottles into a shirt.

The children learned that they were not able to recycle items at school or at home but that they could reuse objects to make new items. A group of students represented the process involved in recycling objects. Other children made new objects by reusing items they had collected.

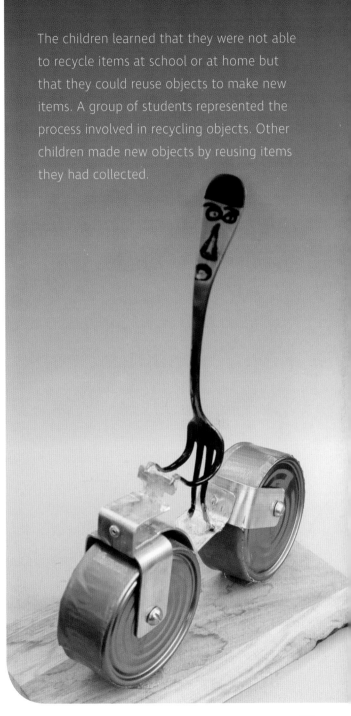

Even though the concept of reducing had not been included in any of their questions, the experts helped the children understand what they could do at school and home to create less waste. As a consequence, many of the children in the class started bringing items for lunch in containers rather than wrapped in plastic, and they also began drawing on both sides of sheets of paper.

As weeks went by, the students in Ms. Mory's class had collected many objects that could be reused, but they did not have a clear idea about what they could do with them. A couple of children in the class commented that the playhouse in the playground was worn down and quite ugly and that they could probably use some of the objects they had collected to make the playhouse prettier. Ms. Mory and her students inspected the playhouse and confirmed that it was in really bad shape. Together, they brainstormed what they could do:

"We can decorate the walls."

"We can make chairs for the children to sit on."

"We can fix the table and make it look nicer."

The whole class wanted to take part in refurbishing the playhouse. Together they brainstormed and made a to-do list. To meet their objectives, the children worked in small groups to make all of the different items. A group of children made a table, and a second group made decorations for the wall. A third group made planters to hang on the window, and a fourth group made chairs out of discarded tires and rope.

Picturing the Project Approach | Creative Explorations in Early Learning

Phase 3—Concluding the Project

After several weeks of collaboration, the children completed their work. They invited other classes to the grand opening of the newly beautified playhouse, which teachers designated for all children to enjoy during their free periods.

Appendix A: Project Planning and Documentation Chart for Project on Fruit

Discussion	Fieldwork	Representation	Investigation	Display
Phase 1—Beginning the Project				
• Teacher shared a personal story about how she likes having fruit for breakfast • Whole fruit was brought in as a provocation for discussion	Parents were asked to send in pictures of children's prior experiences with fruit	• Children made drawings of prior experiences with fruit • Children made memory drawings of fruit	• Does the color of fruit inform you about how it will taste? • Is the size of fruit proportional to the amount of seeds it has? • Are fruits the same color on the inside and outside? • Is the fruit peel edible? • How are fruits consumed? • How do I know if a fruit is ripe?	• Photographs showed children's prior experiences with fruit • Memory drawings depicted different kinds of fruits • Drawings illustrated experiences with fruits
Phase 2—Developing the Project				

• Children reviewed the questions they had to remember to ask the experts
• Along with the teacher, children made sure they had all materials to record the information experts would share
	• Children used their senses to investigate different fruits
	• Children explored whole and cut fruits
	• A mom donated fruit trees, and children saw fruit grow
	• Parents came in to juice fruits; dehydrate fruits; and make fruit cocktail, marmalade, smoothies, freezer pops, and apple pie
		• Children made sketches of their findings when carefully examining fruits
		• Children took notes on their experiences with visiting experts
		• Children made drawings of the steps for the recipes they made
		• Children used varied materials to make 3-D representations of the fruits they explored
		• Children recorded the changes they witnessed in the donated fruit trees
			• Children watched informative videos and read books that could answer their questions
			• New questions arose:
			  • Where else do fruits grow?
			  • Where do we buy fruit?
			  • What are the different parts of fruits?
			  • Why should we eat fruit?
				• A record showed ongoing changes in the fruit trees
				• Children's representations showed the process of change as they gained new knowledge and understanding
				• The teacher posted children's 3-D representations of fruit

Phase 3—Concluding the Project				
With the teacher, children chose representations to show parents the new learning and understanding gained through their investigation	• Children shared their knowledge with peers in the school who did not have the same project experience • Parents reported that children showed more knowledge and curiosity about fruits than before the investigation	• Children chose to share some aspects of their learning with another group in the school • Children chose to share the whole story of the project with parents so they could see children's prior knowledge of fruit and the understanding gained during the investigation	• Can we buy all fruit in the supermarket all year long? • Are there fruits that don't grow in our country?	• The teacher gave a keynote presentation to share the project story with parents • Children made more marmalade for parents at the presentation • Children shared their informative displays with another group of students who were also studying fruits

Appendix B: How to Make a Topic Web

The following guidelines explain how to create a topic web for project work. If desired, teachers may come together in a group to work on their topic webs. Each teacher can work individually, and then all members can share their webs with the group. If teachers work together in a team on the same topic, they have the option to combine their webs as they plan their classroom projects.

Materials

Per person:
- 1 pad of 100 small sticky notes, 1.5" x 2"
- Pencil
- 8.5" x 11" paper
- Space at a large table

Procedure

1. Brainstorm: Individually, write as many words as you can that relate in any way to the topic, using a separate sticky note for each word. Spread the notes on the table as you go. The words should be as specific and concrete as possible.

   Time: about seven minutes

   Tips:

   - Work alone at this stage, even if you plan to team teach.
   - Use visual imagery.
   - Think about aspects of the topic that relate to all of your senses.
   - Think about people whose work is involved with this topic.
   - Resist the temptation to think of abstract categories.

   - Continue for about seven minutes or until you have about fifty or sixty notes.

2. Sort: Arrange the words into groups of items that are alike and different. When you do this, you may find you have very different numbers of items in the groups.

   Time: about five minutes

   Tips:

   - Break down very large groups into subgroups. If you have a group that has only one or two words in it, try to think of some other words that belong.
   - The aim is not to get groups of equal size but to understand the attributes that characterize each group.

3. Label: Write headings or category labels for each group. Choose the word or short phrase that best expresses the concept connecting the items.

   Time: about five minutes

   Tips:

   - You may find that you want to regroup one or two sets of items during this process.
   - You can, of course, add any new ideas that occur to you.
   - You may discover that one of the words in a group is the one you wish to have as the heading for the whole set.
   - For clarity, it is helpful to make the headings look different by using a different-colored paper or pen.

Appendix B (continued)

4. Share: If you are doing this activity together with other teachers, now is the time to look at the ideas and categories in others' webs. This is the kind of collaboration that characterizes useful teamwork.

   Tips:

   • Note the common features; some items and categories will appear in all sets. Some items will be specific to one set and may reveal personal interests or experiences.

   • As you look at each other's work, note any ideas you would like to incorporate into your own web. The idea is not to make the webs identical but to take advantage of each other's best ideas.

5. Transcribe: The final task is to transcribe the groups of words onto one sheet of paper in web format. This format is preferable to any kind of flowchart, because the ideas are represented not in sequential order but as a constellation radiating from a central idea, topic, or theme title.

Tips:

• Write the title of the topic in the center of the paper in a circle.

• Surround it with the group headings.

• Underline the group headings.

• List the items in each group outward from the headings. Any group heading can generate subcategories.

Appendix C: Example Letter Home Introducing a Project

Dear families,

In our first project for this school year, we will study rocks. Children will have the opportunity to explore different kinds of rocks, pebbles, and stones. It is our intention to guide the children in developing their natural creativity and curiosity so that they become observers, inquirers, and, thus, scientists.

I ask you to encourage these skills by helping your child notice the rocks in the environment. I recommend that you do not give your child information. Allow your child to explore and discover. When your child asks questions, respond with another question or comment that will lead your child to devise his or her own predictions. Ask questions or make comments such as the following:

- What do you think?

- What makes you say that?

- That's interesting.

- I hadn't thought of that.

By doing this, you will help your child come up with his or her own explanations, formulate theories, question the environment, and develop thinking skills.

You can enrich our project by kindly suggesting sites where we could carry out fieldwork and experts we could visit or invite to the classroom to speak about the topic. Likewise, we welcome your contributions and suggestions of books, photographs, videos, or websites related to the topic.

We would like to start a class rock collection. Please help your child find an interesting rock to bring to school. Children can share stories telling where they found their rocks. They will also be invited to talk about the similarities and differences they see in the items in our collection. If your child seems interested in a rock that is too big to carry in, you can send a photograph.

Thank you for your support!

Best regards,

Ms. García

Appendix D: Questions, Predictions, and Findings for Project on Fruit

Questions	Predictions	How We Found the Information	Findings
Does the color of fruit inform you about how it will taste?	Red fruits are spicy.	Children tasted different kinds of red fruits.	The color of a fruit does not necessarily give you information on how it tastes.
Is the size of fruit proportional to the amount of seeds it has?	Bigger fruits have more seeds.	The teacher cut open different kinds of fruit, and the children counted the seeds.	The size of a fruit does not necessarily relate to the number of seeds it has.
Are fruits the same color on the inside as on the outside?	Fruits are the same color on the inside as on the outside.	A student's mom came in to make fruit salad. She showed the children each of the fruits to be used. They talked about the color of each fruit before she cut it. Then, she sliced each fruit and talked about the differences in color between the outsides and the insides of the fruits.	Not all fruits are the same color on the inside as on the outside.
Is the fruit peel edible?	The fruit peel is not edible.	An expert came to the classroom and brought in different kinds of fruit. He explained which peels were edible and which were not.	Some fruits have edible peels.
How are fruits consumed?	Fruits are consumed raw.	Parents came into the classroom to interact with the children and use fruit in different ways. Some made orange juice, others made banana bread, and others made apple chips.	Fruits can be consumed raw, cooked, juiced, or dehydrated.
How do I know if a fruit is ripe?	If I touch it and it feels soft, that means it is ripe.	The students visited a farmers' market and looked at a variety of fruits. The expert explained how to choose fruits that are good to eat. Some you can touch; others you can smell; others you can look at to determine whether they are ripe.	Depending on the fruit, there are different factors to consider to determine whether a fruit is ripe, such as smell, size, weight, color, and firmness.

Appendix E: Letter for All Parents Going on Field Trip

Dear parents,

Thank you for taking part in our field trip. As you all know, we have finished the first phase of our plants project. The children have come up with some questions that we will try to have answered at the botanical garden. We have already spoken to the people at the garden, and they know what the children's questions are and what they are especially interested in knowing more about. The whole class will take a guided tour of the botanical garden. After the tour, you will take your group for more detailed investigations.

You will be in charge of a group of four children. It is very important that you help us record information that may be helpful back in the classroom. Also, please note individual students' reactions and interests, and be mindful of what the children say about the experiences they are encountering. For that purpose, you will be given a clipboard, a pencil, and an electronic tablet for taking pictures or videos.

Make sure the children in your group have enough time to look closely at items as they take field notes and make field sketches. Please point out to the children in your group different kinds of plants, sequences of events, processes, people at work, vehicles, materials, equipment, tools, and machines that can be seen at the site. Advise the children on opportunities for counting, measuring, asking new questions, interviewing people, and clarifying new ideas. After getting permission from the botanical-garden staff, suggest to the children some samples they might bring back to the classroom.

Here are the children's questions on the topic:

• How do plants drink water?	• Are plants edible?	• Can plants grow in water?
• What are the parts of a plant?	• What kinds of animals live in plants?	
• What colors are plants?	• Where do plants come from?	

If you see an opportunity for the children to have their questions answered simply by exploring the environment, have them notice what they can investigate. If not, remind them to ask the experts.

Thank you for your support in making this trip a wonderful experience for all of us!

Ms. Green

Appendix F: Letter to Individual Parents Going on Field Trip

Dear Mrs. Peng,

I am excited about our upcoming visit to the botanical garden on Tuesday, and I am grateful that you will be able to accompany us. I ask for your help with the following details.

Please be at school promptly at 9:00 a.m., because the bus will leave at 9:15 a.m.

You will be taking care of and working with Antonio, Rhiannon, James, and Meihui.

Please be sure to take the following supplies, which I will have ready for you and the children in your group: clipboards for the children, small bags for them to collect samples, a pad for you to take notes about their conversations, and an electronic tablet.

When we get to the botanical garden, the whole class will go together on a tour.

After the tour, you and the children in your group will go to the area called Fantastic Forest to take a close look at the trees. Encourage the children to make field sketches and to take notes on items that draw their attention. Collect samples of leaves of different trees, if you find some on the ground. (Please do not pull leaves off the trees.)

While the children are working, take notes on their conversations and comments. I know that children posing and smiling at the camera can be irresistible, but I ask that you photograph the children while they are exploring and taking notes.

We will meet at the exit at noon to board the bus and return to school. Please be sure that you and the children are at the meeting point on time.

I thank you for your enthusiasm and support.

Ms. Green

Appendix G: Letter Inviting Parents to the Culminating Event

Dear families,

Our project on plants has come to a close, and we would like to celebrate the learning the children have achieved. We invite you to our project presentation, during which we will highlight the research children have conducted over the past eight weeks. We will try to re-create for you all of the experiences we had during the investigation and will display the children's work products.

The children would like to share with you the many ways they acquired knowledge and understanding related to their wonderings. We will recount the field visits, the direct exploration of plants, the opportunities to meet with experts, and the research made through technological devices and books.

We thank you for all of the support you gave us by accompanying us to the different field sites we visited, for sharing with us books and other materials on the topic, and for coming in to speak to the class as experts.

We hope to see you at the closing event!

Date: Monday, September 25, 2017

Time: 9:30 a.m.

Place: Ms. Molly's classroom

Appendix H: Social and Emotional Development Opportunities in the Context of a Project

In project work, children develop social and emotional competencies such as working collaboratively, making choices, persisting to accomplish what they set out to do, solving problems, and regulating their emotions. The following table indicates phases in a project and features of the project work that invite and enhance social and emotional development in school.

Project Phase	Discussion	Fieldwork	Representation	Investigation	Display
Phase 1	• Sharing memories in class discussions or in pairs or small groups • Talking about personal experiences related to the topic • Sharing prior knowledge	Talking at home with parents and caregivers about prior experiences related to the topic	• Making representations of personal experiences or knowledge about the topic in pairs or groups • Talking with others about their work	• Asking questions about the topic based on prior knowledge and a desire to find out more about the topic • Sharing curiosity about and interest in the topic	Sharing representations of the topic around the classroom so that other children can see them
Phase 2	• Preparing for a field visit • Predicting what children will see and the experts they may be able to talk to • Reviewing safety procedures and behavior guidelines • Afterward, reviewing what was seen and learned on the field trip and during further explorations • Discussing representations to show a growing understanding of the topic	• Making a visit to a field site outside the classroom • Talking with experts at the site • Asking questions of the field personnel • Learning to behave appropriately and be safe at a field site	• Making field notes and sketches to represent what is seen at the field site and sharing them back in the classroom • Working collaboratively on posters or other complex representations with classmates • Discussing together what makes a successful representation	• After fieldwork, engaging in follow-up investigations, explorations, and experiments in pairs or small groups • Sharing new questions that arise • Consulting secondary sources of information, such as books, videos, and the Internet	• Displaying children's work on the classroom walls • Encouraging children to consult one another's work and to discuss their work with classmates • Helping children understand the significance of all the work—not just their own—that is displayed

Project Phase	Discussion	Fieldwork	Representation	Investigation	Display
Phase 3	• Reviewing the work of the project in discussion with the whole group • Discussing how the work of the project might be shared with another class of children or with families • Considering which work is complete, which needs more attention, and which is still to be started	• Involving a group of others from outside the class in seeing the work that has been done • Delivering invitations to a sharing event • Inviting experts to see the work accomplished	• Summarizing the main achievements of the project for an outside audience • Considering what others might need to know about their work • Adding finishing touches to group work to make it easy to read and understand • Thinking about how to invite the visitors to review the work done	• Considering how others might see their work and finding ways to record what others think • Making comment boxes, checklists, and forms to collect survey data	• Preparing the classroom for visitors who will come to see the work of the project • Making sure that everyone's work is well displayed so that their role in the work of the project can be appreciated

Appendix I: Meeting STEM Objectives through Project Work

Objective	STEM Education	Project Approach
Prior Knowledge	STEM investigations are designed to extend children's prior learning.	Learning experiences build on what children already know and can do.
Inquiry	Science engages children in asking questions.	Children's questions drive the inquiry.
Curiosity	Science involves wondering how things work. Children's sense of curiosity about the world around them is fostered to promote a lifelong interest in learning.	At the core of the project approach lies the belief that children are striving to make better and fuller sense of their experiences and their environment.
Prediction	The scientific method includes predicting the outcome of experiments.	Children are encouraged to develop their own ideas about how things work.
Investigation	Science involves observing and making discoveries. Children are led to answer their own questions.	Children are prompted to acquire firsthand information through fieldwork, by interviewing experts and by consulting other sources of information.
Exploration	During science lessons, children explore, process, and come to understand new information using their five senses.	Children become comfortable with actively and interactively exploring phenomena, objects, materials, processes, and events around them.
Data Gathering	Science requires data gathering.	When carrying out investigations, children learn to anticipate what they will need for gathering and recording the data that they might encounter.
Perspective	Teachers are encouraged to listen with interest to their students and have them listen to each other as well.	Children engage in discussions after sharing an experience, and they often recall different details. They learn from the work of others because it shows them another approach to the topic being studied. Children can revisit the information they have learned from unfamiliar angles so they may check their understanding in different ways.
Invention	Preschool children begin to develop concepts in engineering as they design, build, and test solutions.	Children can express their ideas and understanding through a variety of representations as they learn on their own terms. For example, children may use diagrams and graphic organizers when categorizing, comparing, and contrasting information.

Objective	STEM Education	Project Approach
Reflection	Teachers can discuss STEM experiences and experiments and can interpret the data together with children.	Teachers and children review and evaluate the project work, and they make a point to communicate the learning.
Engagement	The classroom environment is conducive to experimentation, and children are guided to use materials for that purpose.	Children find out how things work, what things are made of, what people around them do to contribute to their well-being, and so on. The explorations hinge on their interests and ideas. The project offers them choices and involves them in decision making.
Learning and Curricular Objectives and Standards	Standards and guidelines establish what young children need to know and be able to do in STEM at different ages. Ideally, teachers implement lessons in ways that are meaningful, relevant, and respectful for each child and family.	Project work fosters the acquisition of knowledge, skills, dispositions, and feelings by having opportunities to discover and interact with content and connect with the disciplines through real-life experiences, thus integrating learning across the curriculum.
Modes of Instruction	Teachers can implement and assess standards in ways that support all young children's development by using a range of instructional methods, including small- and large-group instruction, and by maintaining a focus on play.	The teacher's systematic instruction aids the acquisition of skills. Children's explorations allow them to find ways to apply skills acquired earlier. Children learn not only how to use a skill but also when to use it, which reveals deeper understanding.
Structure	Many early childhood education programs are designed to support integrated STEM learning.	The structure of this approach provides students with a framework that helps them understand what they are expected to do; it guides and organizes the learning process.
Flexibility	Educators can support STEM learning by providing children with sufficient time for explorations.	The five structural features of the project approach provide flexibility by leaving teachers to decide when, where, how often, and in what form to integrate these recurring components.
Technology	Children understand that tools help people do things better or more easily and do some things that otherwise could not be done at all.	Children typically document their interactions with their surroundings using technological equipment. They also use digital media to represent their understanding, reflect on their new knowledge, explore, gather information, and communicate learning.
Connection to Real Life	Helping children develop their mathematical thinking and reasoning abilities through functional experiences can build their capacity to learn math relevant to their lives.	Project work topics are meant to connect what children learn in the classroom with the world outside of school.

References

Alaska Departments of Education and Early Development and Health and Social Services. 2007. *State of Alaska Early Learning Guidelines: A Resource for Parents and Early Educators.* Department of Education and Early Development, Division of Teaching and Learning Support, and the Department of Health and Social Services, Division of Public Assistance. http://education.alaska. gov/publications/earlylearningguidelines.pdf

Bellanca, James. 2010. *Enriched Learning Projects: A Practical Pathway to 21st Century Skills.* Bloomington, IN: Solution Tree.

Chard, Sylvia C. 1998. *The Project Approach: Making Curriculum Come Alive,* Book One. New York: Scholastic.

Chard, Sylvia C. 1998. *The Project Approach: Managing Successful Projects,* Book Two. New York: Scholastic.

Chard, Sylvia C. 2009. *Projects and the Curriculum: Seeing the Possibilities.* A Series of Six Practical Guides for Teachers, Number 1. http://projectapproach.org

Chard, Sylvia C. 2009. *Features of the Project Approach: A Framework for Learning.* A Series of Six Practical Guides for Teachers, Number 2. http://projectapproach.org

Chard, Sylvia C. 2009. *Making a Start on Projects: Planning in Context.* A Series of Six Practical Guides for Teachers, Number 3. http://projectapproach.org

Chard, Sylvia C. 2009. *Phase 1: Launching a Project: Initial Understanding.* A Series of Six Practical Guides for Teachers, Number 4. http://projectapproach.org

Chard, Sylvia C. 2009. *Phase 2: Developing a Project: Investigating and Representing.* A Series of Six Practical Guides for Teachers, Number 5. http://projectapproach.org

Chard, Sylvia C. 2009. *Phase 3: Concluding a Project: Presenting the Work.* A Series of Six Practical Guides for Teachers, Number 6. http://projectapproach.org

Chard, Sylvia C. 2016. "The Project Approach and STEM: A Powerful Combination." Community Playthings. http://www.communityplaythings.com/resources/articles/2016/the-project-approach-and-stem

Helm, Judy Harris. 2015. *Becoming Young Thinkers: Deep Project Work in the Classroom.* New York: Teachers College Press.

Helm, Judy Harris, and Lilian Katz. 2010. *Young Investigators: The Project Approach in the Early Years.* 2nd ed. New York: Teachers College Press.

Katz, Lilian 2010. "STEM in the Early Years." *Early Childhood Research and Practice* 12(2). http://ecrp.uiuc.edu/beyond/seed/katz.html

Katz, Lilian, and Sylvia Chard. 2000. *Engaging Children's Minds: The Project Approach.* 2nd ed. Stamford, CT: Ablex.

Katz, Lilian, Sylvia C. Chard, and Yvonne Kogan. 2014. *Engaging Children's Minds: The Project Approach.* 3rd ed. Santa Barbara, CA: ABC-CLIO.

Laboy-Rush, Diana. 2009. "Integrated STEM Education through Project-Based Learning." Learning.com. http://www.rondout.k12.ny.us/common/pages/DisplayFile.aspx?itemId=16466975

Meyrick, Kristy M. 2011. "How STEM Education Improves Student Learning." *Meridian K-12 School Computer Technologies Journal* 14(1).

"Nurturing STEM Skills in Young Learners, PreK–3." *STEM Smart Brief.*
http://www.successfulstemeducation.org/sites/successfulstemeducation.org/files/STEM%20Smart%20Brief-Early%20
Childhood%20Learning.pdf

Rushton, Stephen, and Anne Juola-Rushton. 2011. "Linking Brain Principles to High-Quality Early Childhood Education." *Exchange*
202: 8–11.

Index

Conceptual language, 13

Conflict resolution, 54, 81–82

Counting skills, 2, 15

Critical-thinking skills, 61

Curriculum standards, 10, 84, 104

    topic webs, 9, 14–15

D

Descriptive language, 15

Developing the project, ii, 2, 25–42, 92

    case examples, 68–72, 78–82, 87–90

Dewey, John, ii

Digital presentations, 47, 68–69, 75

Discussion, 4–6

Display of work, 4–6, 20, 25, 41, 83, 92, 100–101

Documentation, ii, 2, 5, 21, 43–49

    chart, 6, 92

Dramatic play, 15, 20, 36, 80

E

Emotional regulation, 51

Ending the project, 3, 43–49, 92

    case examples, 73–75, 83, 91

Engineering skills, iv

    promoting, 57–62, 102–103

Evaluation, 6, 43–44

Excitement, iii, 21

Expressing ideas, 33–34

F

Families

    as experts, 32

    inviting to the classroom, 46–48, 74–75, 83

    involving, 9, 10, 19, 71–72

social-emotional learning, 100–101

  understanding, 1–7

  vs. thematic units, 1–2, 57–62

Project planning chart, 6, 92

Q

Questioning, 21–23, 31, 54, 58, 61, 66, 78, 86, 92, 96–97, 100, 102

R

Ramírez, Carlos, iv

Reading skills, 2

Reasoning skills, ii

Recording information, 15, 27–30

Recycling, 74, 84–91

Representing knowledge, 4–6, 35–41, 88–89, 92, 100–101

S

Scaffolding, 22

Scientific thinking, 15

promoting, 57–62, 102–103

Secondary sources, 6, 25, 31, 100

Self-esteem, 52

Sensory experiences, 15, 27, 92

Social studies, 15

Social-emotional development, iv, 33–34

  opportunities for, 100

  supporting, 51–55

Sorting skills, 15, 86, 93

Sounds, 21

STEM knowledge, iv

  promoting, 57–62, 102–103

Storytelling, 16–19, 54

T

Teacher's role, 2–5, 55

Teaching to the test, 57

Technology skills, 15

    promoting, 57–62, 102–103

Thematic units

    vs. project approach, 1–2

Tools, iv, 103

    for fieldwork, 28

    to represent knowledge, 35–41

    using, 15

Topic webs, 9, 13–16, 65, 76–77, 84–85

    making, 93–94

Topics

    age-appropriate, 11

    identifying, 9–11

U

Understanding

    baseline, ii, 2–3, 6, 9, 17–18, 66, 100, 102

    building on, 10

    representing, 33–41, 43–49

V

Vocabulary, 13, 15, 80

W

Writing skills, ii–iii, 18–19, 36